Stevenson College Edinburgh.
Library

KT-471-828

Top 25 locator map
(continues on inside
back cover)
←

tyPack
adrid *Top 25*

JONATHAN HOLLAND

AA Publishing

Find out more about AA Publishing and the
wide range of travel publications and services
the AA provides by visiting our website at
www.theaa.com/bookshop

ve any comments
stions for this guide
contact the editor at
theAA.com

About This Book

KEY TO SYMBOLS

🕂 Map reference to the accompanying fold-out map and Top 25 locator map

✉ Address

☎ Telephone number

🕓 Opening/closing times

🍴 Restaurant or café on premises or nearby

🚆 Nearest railway station

🚇 Nearest subway (tube) station

🚌 Nearest bus route

🚢 Nearest riverboat or ferry stop

♿ Facilities for visitors with disabilities

✋ Admission charges: Expensive (over €5), Moderate (€3–5), and Inexpensive (€3 or less)

↔ Other nearby places of interest

❓ Other practical information

► Indicates the page where you will find a fuller description

ℹ Tourist information

ORGANIZATION

This guide is divided into six sections:

- Planning Ahead, Getting There
- Living Madrid—Madrid Now, Madrid Then, Time to Shop, Out and About, Walks, Madrid by Night
- Madrid's Top 25 Sights
- Madrid's Best—best of the rest
- Where to—detailed listings of restaurants, hotels, shops, and nightlife
- Travel Facts—practical information

In addition, easy-to-read side panels provide fascinating extra facts and snippets, highlights of places to visit, and invaluable practical advice.

The colours of the tabs on the page corners match the colours of the triangles aligned with the chapter names on the contents page opposite.

MAPS

The fold-out map in the wallet at the back of this book is a comprehensive street plan of Madrid. The first (or only) map reference given for each attraction refers to this map. **The Top 25 locator maps** found on the inside front and back covers of the book itself are for quick reference. They show the Top 25 Sights, described on pages 26–50, which are clearly plotted by number (**1**–**25**, not page number) across the city. The second map reference given for the Top 25 Sights refers to this map.

Contents

WITHDRAWN
Stevenson College Edinburgh
Bankhead Ave EDIN EH11 4DE

Planning Ahead

WHEN TO GO

Because of its site high on the inland plateau, Madrid can have some of the most extreme weather conditions in central Spain. Spring, early summer, and autumn are the best times to visit. Although tourist crowds dwindle in winter, the weather can be bitterly cold, with temperatures rarely above freezing during the day.

TIME

Spain is six hours ahead of New York, nine hours ahead of Los Angeles, and one hour ahead of the UK.

AVERAGE DAILY TEMPERATURES

JAN	FEB	MAR	APR	MAY	JUN	JUL	AUG	SEP	OCT	NOV	DEC
48°F	52°F	59°F	64°F	70°F	79°F	88°F	86°F	77°F	66°F	55°F	48°F
9°C	11°C	15°C	17°C	21°C	26°C	31°C	30°C	25°C	19°C	13°C	9°C

Spring (March to mid-June) vies with autumn as the most pleasant time of year, with clear skies and sunny days, though there may be showers.

Summer (Mid-June to August) is hot and dry. Rain is unusual between June and October. July and August are particularly hot.

Autumn (September to October) has little rain, warm sunny days, and moderate temperatures.

Winter (November to February) has dry, clear days and low temperatures—it's cold, and snow is not unknown.

WHAT'S ON

January *Cabalgata de Reyes* (5 Jan): A procession marks the Three Wise Men's arrival.

San Antón (17 Jan): Pets are blessed in the San Antón Church, Calle Hortaleza 63.

February *Carnival:* A week of processions and parties ends on Ash Wednesday with the ritual "Burial of the Sardine" by the River Manzanares.

ARCO: International contemporary arts festival.

April *Semana Santa* (Holy Week): Hooded, shoeless, chain-dragging *penitentes*

bear images of Christ and the Virgin on their shoulders. On Holy Thursday during the procession around La Latina, the entire *barrio* takes to the streets.

May *Labour Day* and *Madrid Day* (1–2 May): Concerts region-wide; the main venue is Plaza Mayor.

San Isidro (15 May): Nightly concerts in Plaza Mayor mark the week leading up to the saint's day of San Isidro.

June *St. Antonio* (13 Jun): Street party marks St. Antonio's feast day.

August *Verbenas:* Saint's day celebrations around La Latina and Lavapiés.

September *Festival de Otoño:* International performing arts festival (through November).

Música en las Ventas: Contemporary music in the bullring (through October).

December *Feria de Artesanía:* A craft fair in the Paseo de Recoletos leads up to Christmas. Christmas fair in Plaza Mayor.

New Year's Eve: Thousands gather for the fireworks in the Puerta del Sol.

MADRID ONLINE

www.tourspain.es
The main Spanish tourist board site, strong on Madrid with loads of detail in English on both the city and its environs. Can be slow.

www.munimadrid.es
This site, run by the Ayuntamiento (city council) and aimed primarily at locals, is strong on functional, up-to-date city information and has a good English-language facility.

www.puertademadrid.com
This comprehensive site has information for everyone and covers everything from sightseeing to shopping, entertainment, news, and weather.

www.ctm-madrid.es
Come to terms with getting around Madrid before you arrive by browsing this clear and useful site covering buses and the metro (in English).

www.descubremadrid.com
Site of Madrid's Chamber of Commerce. Has maps, street plans, flight information, an exhibitions' guide, restaurant tips, suggestions for walks, and a business "What's On" section.

http://madrid.lanetro.com
Even a modicum of Spanish will be enough to access probably the best and zappiest of the Spanish-language events and listings sites, covering music, clubs, films, and restaurants.

www.GoMadrid.com
A general-purpose and efficient site covering Madrid and the surrounding area—no surprises, but good for run-of-the-mill information.

www.hotelconnect.co.uk
A good, on-line hotel booking service with a wide range of options in Madrid—if your first choice is fully booked, they'll offer similar quarters in the same price range.

GOOD TRAVEL SITES

www.fodors.com
A complete travel-planning site. You can research prices and weather; book air tickets, cars, and rooms; ask questions (and get answers) from fellow travellers; and find links to other sites.

www.renfe.es/ingles
The official site of Spanish National Railways with an English-language option.

www.wunderground.com
Good weather forecasting.

CYBERCAFÉS

Café Comercial
✉ Gta de Bilbao 7
☎ 91 521 56 55
🕐 Mon–Thu 7.30–1AM, Fri–Sat 8.30–2AM, Sun 10–1AM 🚇 Bilbao.

Ono.com
✉ Gran Via 59 ☎ 91 448 39 52 🕐 24 hours 🚇 Plaza de España.
also at
✉ Fuencarral 121 🚇 Alonso Martinez.

UFO
✉ Princesa 25 ☎ 91 547 89 26 🕐 Mon–Fri 9–9 🚇 Ventura Rodriguez.

Getting There

ENTRY REQUIREMENTS

Anyone entering Spain must have a valid passport (or official identity card for EU nationals). Nationals of Australia and South Africa require a valid passport and a visa. Visa requirements are subject to change, check before making your reservations.

MONEY

The euro is the official currency of Spain. Bank notes in denominations of 5, 10, 20, 50, 100, 200, and 500 euros and coins in denominations of 1, 2, 5, 10, 20, and 50 cents, and 1 and 2 euros, were introduced on 1 January 2002.

€10

€50

€200

€500

ARRIVING

All flights arrive at Barajas Airport, which is 16km (10 mi) east of the city. There are three terminals: T1 for international flights, T2 for national flights and some European flights run by Iberia (the Spanish airline), and T3 for regional flights.

Arriving by Air

For information on Barajas airport ☎ 91 393 60 00; flight information ☎ 90 235 35 70/91 305 83 45. A bus leaves Barajas ⓜ 5AM–2AM every 15 minutes (look for the EMT sign). It arrives at an area directly beneath the Plaza de Colón. The journey takes 30–60 minutes and costs €2. To get from Plaza de Colón to the Colón metro, go up to street level and cross the square, a five-minute walk. The metro (line 8) goes directly to Nuevos Ministerios (journey time 10 minutes) where there is a link to the Cercanía overground suburban lines. A single ticket costs €1.10. A taxi from the airport to the centre of Madrid takes around 20 minutes and costs €20–25.
For Iberia information ☎ 90 240 05 00.

Arriving by Train

Trains from France, Portugal, and northern Spain arrive at Chamartín Station. Trains from southern and eastern Spain and express services from Lisbon arrive at Atocha Station. Both are on the metro system.
Between Chamartín and Atocha are two other stations, Recoletos and Nuevos Ministerios.

ARRIVING BY BUS
Madrid is served from other parts of Spain by many private bus companies. Inter-city coach services arrive at the Estación Sur de Autobuses on Calle Méndez Alvaro, southeast of the city centre. Buses from outside Spain (England, Portugal, and France) also terminate here. For all bus information ☎ 91 468 42 00.

ARRIVING BY CAR
Drivers access Madrid via the Spanish system of toll motorways (*autopistas*) or highways (*autovías*). From France and the north routes run along both the Mediterranean and Atlantic coasts then head towards Madrid; routes through the Pyrenees are slower but more scenic. Madrid is clearly signposted at all interchanges. From southern Spain, take the N-IV from Seville via Córdoba. From Portugal take the N-V from Badajoz. All roads connect with the three ring roads circling Madrid: the M30, M40, and M45. Head for Paseo de la Castellana, Madrid's main artery—most central locations are easily reached from here.

GETTING AROUND
Metro stations are indicated by name and by a diamond-shaped symbol. Services run from 6.30AM until 1.30AM. Single-journey tickets (*sencillo*) are bought at metro stations. *Metrobus* tickets, from newspaper stands and tobacconists, allow 10 metro and/or bus rides. Buses run every 15 minutes from 6AM until midnight. Night buses start in the Plaza de la Cibeles, running every 20 minutes between midnight and 3AM and every hour after that. Flag the bus if it does not look as if it is stopping. Pay the driver or stamp your pass in the machine by the driver's seat. To request a stop, press one of the hard-to-spot red buttons. Taxis are fairly inexpensive. Taxi stands are in key locations, but usually you hail taxis. Take only taxis with a green light on top. Check that the driver has reset the meter. There is a boarding charge and a charge for every kilometre travelled at more than 20kmh (about 12.5mph). For more information ➤ 91.

➤ 91

INSURANCE
Check your insurance coverage and buy a supplementary policy if necessary. EU nationals receive medical treatment with form E111—obtain this form before travelling. Full health and travel insurance is still advised.

VISITORS WITH DISABILITIES
General access in Madrid is patchy but gradually improving. For getting around, buses and taxis are the best bet although only the newest buses have facilities for people with disabilities. New buildings and museums have excellent wheelchair access, older attractions have yet to be converted, and churches are particularly difficult. There is no general guide to accessibility but the Coordinadora de Minusválidos Físicos de Madrid (✉ C/Ríos Rosas 54 ☎ 91 535 06 19 🕒 Mon–Fri 9–3 🚇 Ríos Rosas) co-ordinates information about access and facilities for groups of travellers with disability.

STEVENSON COLLEGE LIBRARY

ACC. No.	A22539	
CLASS/LOC	Spc 914.641	Hol
CAT 28.6.05 AU	PROC	

Living
Madrid

Madrid Now

Above: *taking a stroll through the Plaza Mayor cloisters in Casa de la Panadería*

Madrid lies right in the middle of the Iberian peninsula. Buzzing with life virtually 24 hours a day, it's equally rich in grandiose architecture and comfortable neighbourhoods. More than most European capitals, it preserves a national identity, a quintessential "Spanishness" that has much to do with its allure.

Unlike every other major European capital, Madrid is an invention, an artificial city that was

BARRIOS

• Madrid is divided into 21 *barrios* or neighbourhoods. Logically, the most central part of the city is the centro district. The old quarter, Viejo Madrid, roughly surrounds the Plaza Mayor; the grandiose Barrio de Oriente (Eastern Quarter) fans out around the Palacio Real; and Bourbon Madrid extends outwards along sweeping avenues around the Prado museum. Here you'll find the major sights and museums, plenty of hotels, restaurants, and bars, and some of Madrid's quirkier shopping areas. To the south of the Puerta del Sol is known as the *barrio popular*, or "people's quarter," a picturesque maze of winding streets. Further south are the poorer *barrios* of Arganzuela and Moratalaz. To the east of the Paseo del Prado, the Paseo de Recoletos, and the Paseo de la Castellana is the 19th-century barrio Salamanca. It is these areas, together with the Retiro and Chamberí *barrios*, south and northwest respectively, that are home to the wealthier *madrileños*, residents of Madrid.

A PASSION FOR FOOTBALL

• Football is a Madrid passion. Real Madrid, the most successful of the city's teams, is based at the Santiago Bernabeu Football Stadium, on Paseo de la Castellana, which holds over 80,000 spectators and is used for cup finals and international games. For atmosphere, though, the Vicente Calderón–home of Madrid's rival team, Atlético–is a good bet.

established as a permanent power base for the monarchy by Philip II as late as 1561. Why he chose Madrid is a mystery—it's not on a navigable river and had no cathedral or university —but it was established as the capital and slowly, slowly, it evolved into today's ebullient metropolis. Given its history, much becomes clear. You won't find much Moorish architecture or many medieval buildings in Madrid, because the city scarcely existed before the 16th century. Its big civic showcase buildings and boulevards date from the 17th and 18th centuries, its vibrant working-class neighbourhoods from the 19th. The 20th century saw a modern infrastructure put in place, while the last decades of the second millennium saw Spain re-entering mainstream Europe after the isolation of the Franco years. The economy boomed, while the reappearance of democracy and free speech were the impetus for the creativity and *joie de vivre* in the late 1970s and '80s known as the *Movida* (Shift). Its effect was to create the vivacious, but essentially uniquely Spanish city you find today.

Getting around is easy; Madrid's districts are surprisingly close to one another and the

Above left: the monument to Alfonso XII in the Parque del Retiro

Above: *Colección Thyssen-Bornemisza houses a wide collection of fine art*

SUMMER IN THE CITY

• *Madrileños* leave the city to escape the worst of the summer heat, so from mid-July you'll find many bars and restaurants shut. However, most sights and museums stay open. And the street life after dark is lively, especially at the *terrazas*, or terrace bars. The city also sponsors a summer entertainment programme, *Los Veranos de la Villa*.

pedestrianization of streets around the Palacio Real has made walking a real pleasure. Further afield, and easily reached by the efficient metro system, are other museums and some tempting shopping streets. All over the city you'll find parks and gardens, welcome oases in what can be the blistering heat of summer. Plan ahead if you like sightseeing, or simply want to wander through the different *barrios*. Madrid is not over-burdened with foreign visitors for much of the year, so it's easy to escape the hordes.

Madrileños are another matter—not for nothing does Madrid have the reputation as a city that never sleeps. It's a real revelation to first-time visitors to find the streets as busy at midnight as during the day, and a normal dinner time of 10

Above: *enjoying a few minutes' peace to read the paper in the Palacio Real grounds*
Left: *soak up the vibrant atmosphere along the bustling Gran Vía*
Below left: *"Maravilla's" flamenco shop has dresses of every imaginable colour*

or 11 takes a bit of getting used to. The flip side of this is Madrid's atmosphere, a lively mix of anything-goes, tolerance, and gaiety. Until recently it was one of Europe's most homogeneous capitals, though immigration from Africa, Asia, and South America, plugging gaps in the labour market, has bought diversity. Still, the city seems firmly Spanish. The city fathers

THE *SIESTA*

- The *siesta*, an anomalously old-fashioned habit in a city trying so hard to be modern, looks stubbornly set to stay. You may be frustrated at finding so many shops and museums closed for two hours or more at lunchtime. To enjoy Madrid to the full, it is best to try to adapt–join them in their *siesta* and then again at 1AM on a weekday morning when every central bar is full of people of all ages chatting away. People eat late and go to bed late. Yet as businesses try to march in lockstep with the rest of northern Europe even the *siesta* has become threatened. As a result *madrileños* are functioning on less and less sleep, a fact generating great interest–and worry–for Spanish health watchdogs.

WHAT A NOISE

- Be prepared for a major assault on your ears in Madrid. That's because the city rarely sleeps, natives all seem to talk at the top of their voices, and loud music rules. It's also a city constantly under change. Construction works are going on all over, mainly associated with road and metro extensions. And large-scale renovations that temporarily block off whole squares engender the thump of heavy machinery almost everywhere.

CALLE DEL
CARMEN

Above: *thousands of people watching a bullfight at Plaza de Toros de las Ventas*
Centre right: *street sellers at the extremely popular El Rastro flea market*
Far right: *lush green plants at the Real Jardín Botánico*

actively encourage traditional Spanish culture, and much of the population still lives downtown rather than in the suburbs. Life in Madrid still revolves around café and bar culture; streetlife remains vibrant, and, given the Spanish tradition of spending time in groups, it's unlikely this will change.

The moment may come when, like the natives, you feel the need to escape the crowds and noise, and Madrid is blessed both with its green

---

OLD-FASHIONED HYGIENE

- One of the delights of Madrid is the number of bars and shops with tiled walls—classic Hispano-Moorish designs, wonderfully vibrant and colourful depictions of the owner's trade, his home town, or family life. These *azulejos* date from the late 19th to early 20th centuries and were originally simply cheap and hygienic wall coverings.

city spaces and with accessible outlying towns and monuments. A trip out from the city to visit El Escorial or Aranjuez, where *madrileños* flock on summer weekends, or historic Toledo, makes a great change of pace and a chance to put the city itself into perspective. It's also an opportunity to see the arid and lonely beauty of the *meseta*, the inland plateau, on which Madrid stands.

Coming to Madrid is exhilarating, and it should be a pleasure, not a history lesson or cultural marathon. Soak up the atmosphere; it will stay with you far longer than the memory of yet another painting by Goya or Velázquez. Explore the different *barrios*: each is unique. Poke about in the markets and old-fashioned shops. And do some people-watching in a bar: It's the best way to get a handle on the character of the city. It's up to you to pick and choose what appeals and get your own, unforgettable impression of Madrid.

MADRID'S GRAND AVENUE

● The Gran Vía was created in 1910 when 14 streets were swept away to provide a 20th-century boulevard for motor traffic—and a chance for Madrid to embrace architectural modernity. It slashes across town, its buildings architectural lessons from every decade of the last century, from early French-inspired buildings through modernist structures of the 1920s to the ornate skyscrapers of the Franco years.

15

Madrid Then

Above: *engraving of Alfonso XII and Alfonso VIII.*
Above right: *Napoleon*
Above middle: *the early stages of the Civil War*
Above far right: *crowds reading about Franco's death*

BEFORE AD 800

Iberian tribes inhabited Madrid from around 1000 BC. The Romans ruled the Iberian peninsula between 218 BC and the 5th century AD and Madrid became a stopping place. In AD 711 Muslims defeated the Visigoths—areas of Spain came under Muslim rule for 800 years.

METRO CONNECTIONS

Many of Madrid's metro stations are named after historical figures unknown outside Spain. Among the better known are Colón (Christopher Columbus), Goya, and Velázquez.

854 Muhammad I of Córdoba founds the city of Madrid.

1085 Madrid is recaptured by Alfonso VI; Christians, Jews, and Muslims inhabit the city.

1202 Alfonso VIII recognizes Madrid as a city by giving it Royal Statutes.

1309 The *Cortes*, or Parliament, meets in Madrid for the first time.

1469 The marriage of Catholic monarchs Ferdinand and Isabella unites Aragon and Castile.

1492 The conquest of Granada completes the unification of Spain. Spain begins a 200-year period of imperial power, and expels the Jews.

1561 Philip II establishes Court in Madrid: a cultural "Golden Age" begins.

1598 Philip III (1598–1621) is the first monarch to be born in Madrid.

1617–19 Plaza Mayor is built.

1759 Charles III begins a modernization schedule for Madrid.

1808–12 French occupation; famine kills 30,000. Spanish rule restored 1814.

1819	Prado museum opens; houses are numbered, and streets are named.
1851	The Madrid–Aranjuez railway line is inaugurated.
1873	The Republic is declared.
1917	Spain faces a general strike.
1919	The first metro line in Madrid opens.
1931	The Second Republic is declared.
1936–39	The Spanish Civil War takes place, sparked by uprising in North Africa. The long dictatorship of General Franco follows.
1975	General Franco dies; King Juan Carlos is declared his successor.
1977	The first democratic general election.
1986	Spain joins the EEC (now EU).
1992	Madrid is European City of Culture.
2002	Spain adopts the euro: a landmark in the move to mainstream Europe.
2004	Madrid's bid to stage the 2012 Olympics is overshadowed by train bomb attacks.

MADRID PEOPLE

Charles III

Charles III is often known as "the best mayor that Madrid ever had." More than any other single historical figure, he is responsible for today's Madrid. He came to the throne in 1759 and was a keen proponent of Enlightenment ideals.

Cervantes

Cervantes is the author of *Don Quixote*, believed by some to be the first novel ever written. A tax collector, he wrote *Don Quixote* while in jail for manipulating accounts. He died in Madrid in 1616.

Goya

Goya (1746–1828) is the painter most readily associated with Madrid, though he neither was born nor died here. He settled in Madrid in 1774 and became Court painter to Charles IV in 1789.

Time to Shop

Below: *window-shopping at Plaza de España*
Below right: *looking for bargains at El Rastro flea market*

Since the 1980s out-of-town malls have sprung up and international chains have crept in. But fears that late 20th-century shopping practices would kill off Madrid's many unique little stores have been largely unfounded, and the range of shopping experiences available for visitors is

WHERE TO SHOP

Ask a *madrileño* where to find the city's shopping heart and the answer is bound to be around Calle Preciados, the pedestrianized drag that connects Puerta del Sol with the Gran Vía. Here you'll find branches of all the big chain stores as well as Madrid's biggest department store, and everything from fashion to food. Smarter by far are the quiet, well-heeled streets of the Salamanca district, home to the big designer names and luxury stores of all description. The best places to trawl for souvenirs are around the Plaza Mayor and the surrounding Los Austrias district, or Malasaña. Head for Chueca for cutting-edge style and street fashion.

wonderfully diverse. It's these contrasts between the best on the international scene with some superbly idiosyncratic outlets that makes Madrid shopping so serendipitous.

It's not just what shops sell that provides a contrast—how they look is also varied. Temples of consumerism in steel and glass happily rub shoulders with cramped, dark shops where the stock is piled high and the merchandise specialized beyond belief. Few other world capitals have as many stores devoted to so many oddities—outsize corsetry, plaster statuary, crystallized violets. This gives Madrid shopping a special appeal, whether you're after easy-to-carry souvenirs or seriously self-indulgent retail therapy, or you simply enjoy window-shopping.

Madrid has branches of some of Spain and Europe's best-known fashion stores, as well as the latest in the stylish, chain-store fashion, for which Spain is renowned. Spanish leather shoes, bags, and belts are some of the best in Europe, and excellent value.

Below: *a selection of colourful fruit and veg for sale*
Bottom: *detail of designer shopping bags*
Below left: *the shopping street of Calle de Serano*

ADOLFO DOMINGUEZ

For gifts, you'll find goods from all over Spain, ranging from the tasteful fringed and embroidered shawls and *mantillas*, warm winter capes, elegant hats, delicate china, traditional ceramics, and damascene work, to the marvellously tacky (plastic flamenco dolls, a poster of a *torero* with your name on it, and metal Don Quixotes).

Food makes a great souvenir or gift. In addition to the obvious olive oil, nougat, or chocolate, hunt down saffron, wonderful dried nuts, seeds, and the fruits so loved by the Spanish. Or look for convent-baked biscuits or cakes, or vacuum-packed *jamón* (dry-cured ham), *chorizo* (spicy sausage), or *morcilla* (unctuous black pudding).

Left: *Calle de Serano*

MARKETS

Markets are not only a window into everyday life but also the perfect place to pick up a picnic to eat in the park. Some of the best are La Cebada (🚇 La Latina)–for a huge range of goods and low prices; San Miguel (🚇 Sol)–a stone's throw from the Plaza Mayor; and La Paz (🚇 Serrano)– quality and varied produce aimed at the prosperous Salamanca inhabitants.

19

Out and About

GUIDED CITY TOURS

Julia Tours
➕ bI; D8 ✉ Gran Vía 68
☎ 91 559 96 05
🕐 Mon–Sat 8–8; Sun
8–noon 🚇 Santo
Domingo

Madrid Vision
➕ cII; D9 ✉ Puerta del
Sol ☎ 91 767 1888
💡 One ticket allows you
to get on and off as often
as you wish

Pullmantour
➕ aIII; C9 ✉ Plaza de
Oriente 8 ☎ 91 541 18
05/6/7 🚇 Opera

INFORMATION

ARANJUEZ & CHINCHÓN
Distance 45km (28 mi)
Journey Time 45 minutes
🚌 ALSA from Estación
Sur, Méndez Alvaro
🚆 Cercanías Line or the
Tren de la Fresa (➤ 60)
💡 Expensive
ℹ Plaza San Antonio
☎ 91 891 04 27

EL ESCORIAL
Distance 40km (25 miles)
Journey Time 45 minutes
☎ 91 890 59 03/4
🕐 Tue–Sun 10–6;
Oct–Mar 10–5 (last
admission 1 hour before
closing)
🚆 Regular trains from
Atocha
💡 Expensive

EXCURSIONS
ARANJUEZ & CHINCHÓN

Aranjuez was the Spanish Bourbon monarchy's attempt to create a Spanish Versailles. Inside the palace, highlights are the Porcelain Room, the Throne Room, and the Smoking Room. The

gardens, laid out in the 16th century, include El Jardín de la Isla (Island Garden), crisscrossed with shady walkways. At the far end stands the Casa del Labrador (Peasant's House), built for Charles IV. Nearby Chinchón has a 15th-century castle and a wonderful Plaza Mayor, lined with balconied houses. There is a Goya panel in the Assumption Church. Chinchón is the home of the eponymous *anise* liqueur.

EL ESCORIAL

Philip II's vast palace and monastery was built between 1563 and 1584 as his mausoleum. It contains 16 courtyards, 2,673 windows, 1,200 doors, and 86 staircases; 900m (2,952ft) of frescoes line the walls. Its power is breathtaking, and the clear mountain air has left its granite and blue roof slates looking extraordinarily new. Among the highlights are the monastery, the library, and the mausoleum, the resting place of most Spanish monarchs since Charles V. Further north is the controversial Valle de los Caídos, built by Republican prisoners. It is Franco's resting place and a monument to the victims of the Civil War.

SEGOVIA

Segovia was founded during the Iberian period and taken by the Romans in 80 BC. Occupied by the Moors, it then reverted to the Christians in 1085, and now, a millennium later, it is a popular weekend destination for *madrileños* in search of

fresh air and a traditional suckling pig lunch. The first thing you will see is the Roman aqueduct (1st and 2nd centuries AD), with 165 arches and a total length of 814m (2,670ft). In the old town are the magnificent 16th-century cathedral and the 14th-century Alcázar, or fortress, from the top of which there are lovely views. Segovia is well-known as the capital of Castillian cuisine.

TOLEDO

Legendary Toledo, with its hilltop site and fascinating maze of winding streets and hidden patios, one of the nation's most beautiful and legendary cities, was the Spanish capital from 567 to 711, and from 1085 to 1561. In other words, it has played a decisive role in Spanish history for far longer than Madrid. Between the 12th and 15th centuries Moors and Christians lived there side by side, and its rich combination of Moorish, Christian, and Jewish heritage inspired its designation as a National Monument. Highlights are the 13th-century cathedral, the synagogues, Santo Tomé, the Museo de la Santa Cruz (for El Greco paintings), and the Alcázar, or fort, founded in 1085.

INFORMATION

SEGOVIA
Distance 88km (55 mi)
Journey Time 2 hours
🚌 La Sepulvedana bus line from Paseo de la Florida 11, near Príncipe Pío metro station
🚃 From Chamartín station (very slow)
🍴 Candido, Plaza Azoguejo 5; Restaurante La Almuraza, Calle Marqués del Arco 3
ℹ Plaza Mayor 10
☎ 921 46 60 70; the office on Plaza Azoguejo offers information on the surrounding region
☎ 921 46 03 34

Far left: *the Jardin de la Isla, at the palace of Aranjuez*
Middle: *the slated turrets of the Alcazar at Segovia*
Above: *Palacio de San Lorenzo el Real de El Escorial*

INFORMATION

TOLEDO
Distance 50km (31 mi)
Journey Time 1 hour 15 minutes
🚌 Galeano International from Estación Sur, Méndez Alvaro
🚃 From Atocha, several every hour in summer, less frequent in winter. To avoid a steep climb take a bus up the hill.
ℹ Puerta Bisagra
☎ 925 22 08 43

Stevenson College Edinburgh
Bankhead Ave EDIN EH11 4DE

Walks

INFORMATION

Distance 6.5km (4 mi)
Time 3–4 hours
Start point
★ Puerta del Sol
🅷 cII; D9
🚇 Sol (lines 1, 2, 3)
🚌 3, 5, 15, 20, 51, 52, 150, and others
End point Puerta del Sol

EAST FROM SOL

Start on the Puerta del Sol. Exit at its eastern end and walk down Calle San Jerónimo, through the Plaza de las Cortes, as far as the Neptune fountain in the Plaza de Canovas de Castillo. Turn right down the Paseo del Prado, cross it half-way down, and visit the Jardin Botánico behind the Prado. Now walk down beside the right side of the Prado, then turn right on Calle Felipe IV, walk up past the Casón del Buen Retiro to cross Calle de Alfonso XII and enter the Retiro Park through the Felipe IV gate. Walk through the parterre gardens and up the steps at the end. When you reach the lake, turn left and follow its edge, with the Alfonso XII monument opposite you.

Exit the park at the Puerta de Alcalá and walk up Calle Serrano past the Archaeological Museum. Cut through the Jardines del Descubrimiento, then turn left down the Paseo de Recoletos, parallel to Serrano. When you reach Barbara de Braganza, turn right and walk up past the Plaza de las Salesas. A little way past the church on the right is Calle del Barquillo, an intriguing backstreet shopping area. Go all the way down until you come to the Calle de Alcalá. Turn right and, keeping to your right, walk along the Gran Vía as far as the metro station. Then turn left down Calle de Montera and you are back in Sol.

Barbarade Braganza

Archaeological Museum

Gran Vía

Royal Language Academy

Puerta de Alcalá

Alfonso XII Statue

Parque del Retiro

Jardin Botánico

Plaza de Canovas de Castillo

WEST FROM SOL

Leave the Puerta del Sol at the western end and walk up Calle de Postas to Plaza Mayor. Cross the plaza and leave it at the diagonally opposite corner (El Arco de los Cuchilleros). At the bottom of the steps cross the street and go down Calle del Maestro de la Villa into the Plaza Conde de Barajas. Explore the streets in this area, and come up into the Plaza de la Villa.

Cross Calle Mayor and walk down as far as Calle San Nicolás. Walk up the street, across Plaza Ramales and continue up Calle Lepanto to the Plaza de Oriente. Turn left along the side of Oriente to Calle Bailén, with the Palacio Real across the square ahead of you. Turn right along Bailén, and continue until you see Plaza de España on your right. Take the walkway under Calle Bailén, then walk up the steps to Templo de Debod for the views. Descend the slope at the far end of Templo de Debod and cross the car park for a path down through the Parque del Oeste to the Rosaleda. At Paseo del Rey, turn left and follow it as far as Cuesta de San Vicente. Turn right down to the Puerta de San Vicente, then left into the Paseo de la Virgen del Puerto. On the left, 150m (492ft) down, is the entrance to the Campo del Moro, with the best views of the Royal Palace.

INFORMATION

Distance 5km (3 mi)
Time 2–3 hours
Start point
★ Puerta del Sol
🚇 cII; D9
🚇 Sol (lines 1, 2, 3)
🚌 3, 5, 15, 20, 51, 52, 150 and others
End point Campo del Moro
🚇 C9
🚇 Opera/Príncipe Pío
🚌 3, 25, 39, 148, 500

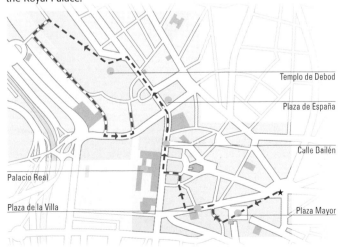

Templo de Debod

Plaza de España

Calle Bailén

Palacio Real

Plaza de la Villa

Plaza Mayor

Madrid by Night

Left: Gran Vía illuminated at night in the "city that rarely sleeps"

Right: a Victoria Duende dancer performing with the "Corral de la Morerie" flamenco show

FLOODLIT STONE

Great cities look wonderful under floodlights and Madrid is no exception. Imaginative lighting enhances much of the centre after dark. Don't miss the subtly lit charms of the Plaza Mayor, then enjoy the brilliance lighting adds to the Palacio Real and the Plaza de Oriente. The Paseo del Prado is beautifully illuminated at night; admire the sparkle of light on the water of the fountains in Plaza de Cibeles and Plaza de Canovas de Castillo before stopping at one of the summertime *terrazas*.

MUSIC, THEATRE, DANCE, AND FILM

Madrid has a year-round agenda of cultural evening events, from opera, orchestral concerts, theatre, dance, and original-language films to jazz, flamenco, and Latin American music. Get information in the weekly entertainment guide *Guía del Ocio* or the monthly English language *InMadrid* (see below), and reserve tickets for concerts and theatre via www.entradas.com (☎ 90 222 16 22) or Localidades Galicia (☎ 91 531 27 32; www.eol.es/lgalicia) ticket lines.

DOING YOUR OWN THING

If you're looking for a low-key evening, it's worth remembering that there's little hope of a restaurant dinner before 9. So you might want to take your evening stroll before you eat. Touristy though it surely is, the Plaza Mayor looks great by night; from here you can wander through buzzing Huertas down to the wide Paseo del Prado, a wonderful place in summer for a stroll and a drink at a *terraza*. A few minutes' walk away lies the Retiro Park, perfect on balmy evenings. For window-shopping, head for the elegant streets of Salamanca or Chueca.

NIGHT OWLS

Madrid's reputation as an all-night party town is deserved. The club scene is constantly evolving. Check out what's what in the free English-language listings magazines, *InMadrid* or *The Broadsheet*. Nightlife concentrates around Huertas, Lavapiés, and Malasaña with more action off Sol. Gay-oriented Chueca is seriously cool and Salamanca is for a dressed-up occasion.

MADRID's
top 25 sights

The sights are shown on the maps on the inside front cover and inside back cover, numbered **1**–**25** across the city

Ermita de San Antonio

HIGHLIGHTS

- Cupola
- Balustrade
- Marble and stucco font (1798)
- *Lápida de Goya*
- Mirrors under the cupola
- High altar
- Lamp under the cupola (18th century)
- *Inmaculada*, Jacinto Gómez Pastor
- *San Luis and San Isidro*, Jacinto Gómez Pastor

INFORMATION

- ✚ B8; locator map off A2
- ✉ Glorieta de San Antonio de la Florida 5
- ☎ 91 542 07 22
- ◷ Tue–Fri 10–2, 4–8; Sat and Sun 10–2. Closed public hols
- ▣ Príncipe Pío
- ▤ 41, 46, 75
- ▤ Norte Station
- ♿ None
- ▥ Inexpensive. Free Wed and Sun
- ↔ Parque del Oeste (▶ 27)
- ❓ Guide book sold at entrance

Goya is surely the painter that most *madrileños* want to claim as their own. The San Antonio de la Florida Hermitage, a National Monument, is a fine memorial to his memory.

Resting place Both church and hermitage—the latter to the left as you face the two buildings—are off the beaten track but worthwhile both for their intimacy and to view Goya's frescoes, recently restored. The original hermitage was begun in 1792 by Charles IV's Italian architect, Francisco Fontana, on the site of a previous hermitage. Goya's remains were buried here in 1919, unfortunately without his head: it is said that it was stolen by scientists who wished to study it.

The frescoes Painted using a technique that was revolutionary at the time, the frescoes are distinguished by their richness of colour. They tell the life of Saint Anthony, representing the saint raising a murdered man from the dead to enable him to name his murderer and spare the life of the innocent accused. The models for the frescoes were members of the Spanish Court, but include other, less reputable figures—placing rogues alongside the Court officials has been seen as indicating Goya's contempt for the Court of the time.

Girlfriends and boyfriends The San Antonio Hermitage is locally considered particularly *castizo* (of the people), and it is the focal point of a peculiar ritual. Saint Anthony is the patron saint of sweethearts; every 13 June, girls come here to pray for a boyfriend. Thirteen pins are placed inside the font; when the girls put their hands into the font, the number of pins that stick indicates how many beaux they will have that year.

Parque del Oeste

Less frequented and more informal than the Retiro, the Parque del Oeste is the best place in the city for a peaceful twilight stroll in summer, particularly at the quieter northern end.

Rubbish dump to park Designed in the first years of the 20th century by landscape gardener Cecilio Rodríguez on what had previously been an immense rubbish heap, the Parque del Oeste was practically destroyed during the Civil War, when it provided a cover for the Republicans as the Nationalist troops invaded Madrid. Now rebuilt, it is still one of the city's most appealing and romantic open spaces, despite the best efforts of litter louts and graffiti artists. The park contains birch, fir, atlas cedar, and cypress trees, among others, as well as a 17,000sq-m (183,000sq-ft) rose garden, La Rosaleda, which hosts a rose festival each May. There are also several statues, including the 1952 Juan Villanueva fountain in the Paseo de Camoens. A *teleférico* (cable car) in the park runs out to the Casa de Campo, affording bird's-eye views over the west of Madrid. In summer, elegant, noisy terrace bars are set up along the Paseo de Pintor Rosales, Ernest Hemingway's favourite street.

Templo de Debod It is somehow typical of Madrid that one of its oddest and most interesting attractions should not be Spanish at all. The Debod Temple, on the site of a former military barracks in a little park of its own at the park's southern corner near Plaza de España, is a 4th-century Egyptian temple honouring the god Amon. It was installed in 1970 as a gift from the Egyptian government to Spanish engineers and archaeologists who had saved many valuable artistic treasures before large areas of land were flooded after the completion of the Aswan Dam.

HIGHLIGHTS

- Templo de Debod
- *Teleférico*
- La Rosaleda
- Fuente (fountain)
- Statue of Juan de Villanueva
- Statue of Sor Juana Inés de la Cruz
- Statue of Simón Bolivar
- View over Casa de Campo
- Trees, including atlas cedar, cypress, and magnolia

INFORMATION

- B7; locator map off A1
- Jardines del Paseo del Pintor Rosales
- 91 409 61 65
- Templo de Debod:
  (91 541 74 50)
  Apr–Sep Tue–Fri 10–2, 6–8, Sat and Sun 10–2; Oct–Mar Tue–Fri 9.45–1.45, 4.15–6.15, Sat and Sun 10–2. Closed Mon and public hols.
  Teleférico:
  (91 541 74 50) Sat, Sun and public hols 12–7
- Argüelles
- 74, 84, 93
- Templo de Debod: Inexpensive. Free Wed and Sun
- Ermita de San Antonio (► 26)

Top: the Debod Temple

Museo de América

HIGHLIGHTS

- Sculptures of people with physical defects (Area 3)
- Canoe and tepee (Area 3)
- Statues of tribal chieftains (Area 3)
- Painting of *Entrance of Viceroy Morcillo into Potosí* (Area 3)
- Shrunken heads (Area 4)
- Mummy of Parácas (Area 4)
- Treasure of the Quimbayas (Area 4)
- "Day of the Dead" paraphernalia (Area 4)
- Trocortesiano Maya Codex (Area 5)

INFORMATION

- ✚ C6; locator map off A1
- ✉ Avenida Reyes Católicos 6
- ☎ 91 549 26 41
- 🕐 Tue–Sat 9.30–3; Sun and public hols 10–3
- Ⓜ Moncloa
- 🚌 Circular, 82, 83, 84
- 🎫 Inexpensive. Free Sun
- ♿ Excellent

Vessel from Peru

You may see this attractive museum either as an attempt to promote international understanding or as propaganda for the Spanish Conquest. None the less it makes a unique contribution to Spanish cultural life.

History Situated on the edge of Madrid's sprawling University City area, and devoted to the presentation and explication of Pre-Columbian and Hispanic artefacts from Latin America, the America Museum is the best place in Spain to absorb the flavour of the culture of a different continent. The collection was housed in part of the Archeological Museum until 1993, when it took its present form. Tragically, much of the material brought back between Columbus' first voyage and the mid-17th century was destroyed in fires, and most of the exhibits were brought to Spain by scientists, or given as donations.

Layout Audio-visual aids are available in Spanish; the only information in English is a small pamphlet available at the entrance. Do yourself a favour and follow the suggested route, as it is easy to get confused and have a less enjoyable experience. The collection is spread over two floors and five areas with different themes: the tools of understanding, the reality of America's society, religion, and communication. Two particular highlights are the Treasure of the Quimbayas (Area 4), including exquisite gold figures, skullcap helmets, drinking flasks, and trumpets from Columbia, and the Trocortesiano Maya Codex (Area 5), which records the arrival of the Spaniards in the New World and the Spanish Conquest in minute, intricate runes.

Museo Cerralbo

Idiosyncratic and intermittently splendid, this curiosity shows you how the nobility of Madrid lived 100 years ago, and in particular highlights the extravagant personality of the fascinating Marquis de Cerralbo.

Home life When you seen the two-floor, late 19th-century home of the 17th Marquis of Cerralbo from the outside it looks rather unpromising. But the clutter of artefacts inside is fascinating, and uniquely among the house-museums in Madrid, the collections are rivalled by the architecture and decor of the rooms themselves, ranging from the frankly shabby to the magnificent. Politician, man of letters, and collector, the Marquis donated the house and its contents to the state in 1922, stipulating that his collection be displayed exactly as he had left it. This is a unique opportunity to see a near-intact aristocrat's home of the turn of the 20th century.

The collection A magnificent grand staircase by Soriano Fort is to your right as you enter. On the second floor the most notable exhibit is El Greco's striking *Ecstasy of St. Francis* (1600–1605) in the chapel. In the gallery surrounding the patio, there are works by José de Ribera and Alonso Cano as well as some haunting Alessandro Magnasco landscapes. On the third floor, there are collections of Western and oriental weaponry, a dining room containing a remarkable Frans Snyders painting, and an appealingly homey library. Pride of place is given to the sumptuous, mirrored ballroom on the first floor, which displays the Marquis' Saxon porcelain as well as intricately engineered clocks, including one particularly fascinating and huge specimen. Note that tours and information are in Spanish only.

HIGHLIGHTS

- Grand staircase
- *Ecstasy of St. Francis*, El Greco
- *Jacob with his Flock*, José de Ribera
- *Devotion*, Alonso Cano
- *Immaculate Conception*, Francisco Zurbarán
- *Porcupines and Snakes*, Frans Snyders
- Sword collection from the courts of Louis XV and XVI
- Monumental mystery clock

INFORMATION

- ✚ C8; locator map A1
- ✉ Calle Ventura Rodríguez 17
- ☎ 91 547 36 46
- 🕐 Jul–Aug: Tue–Sat 10–2, Sun 10.30–1.30; Sep–Jun: Tue–Sat 9.30–3, Sun 10–3
- 🚇 Ventura Rodríguez, Plaza de España.
- 🚌 1, 46, 74, 75
- 🎫 Inexpensive. Free Sun and Wed
- ↔ Parque del Oeste (➤ 27)
- ♿ Few

Top: *the Salón de Baile*

Catedral la Almudena

DID YOU KNOW?

- Almudaina means "small walled city" in Arabic
- Almudit means "grain store"
- Alfonso XII laid the first stone in 1883
- Crypt is built of stone from Portugal
- Image of the Virgin is made of pinewood
- There are 600 columns in the crypt
- Partly built with money from noble families buying their own chapels
- There are 20 chapels: 9 on the right, 11 on the left
- On the crypt floor some blank tombstones still await an owner

INFORMATION

- ✚ all; C9; locator map A3
- ✉ Calle Bailén. Next to Palacio Real
- ☎ 91 548 09 30
- 🕐 Daily 10–1.30, 6–8
- Ⓜ Opera
- 🚌 3, 31, 148
- 🎫 Free
- ↔ Palacio Real (➤ 31), Plaza de Oriente (➤ 32)
- ♿ None

Though not the loveliest cathedral, it reflects years of Spanish architectural thought. The mixture of styles shows how relaxed *madrileños* have been about this building, which you would expect to have been a priority.

A long delay A little over a decade ago, Madrid lacked a cathedral, incredible though it may seem. The first plans for the Almudena, constructed on what was formerly the site of Muslim Madrid's principal mosque, were drawn up in 1879 under Alfonso XII by the architect Giambattista Sacchetti. Redesigned in 1883, it is based on the pattern of a 13th-century cathedral, with a chancel similar to the one at Rheims. A neoclassical style was introduced into the design in 1944 by architect Fernado Chueca Goitia. It wasn't until 1993, when the final touches were added, that the cathedral was consecrated by the Pope. In May 2004 the Almudena provided a spendid backdrop for the wedding of Prince Felipe, heir to the Spanish throne, to Doña Letitia Ortiz Rocasolano. The main entrance is opposite the Royal Palace, the entrance to the crypt along La Cuesta de la Vega.

The story of the Almudena Virgin According to legend, the image of the Virgin over the entrance had been hidden in the 11th century by Mozarabs (Jews and Christians living under Moorish rule). When Spanish hero El Cid reconquered Madrid and drove the Moors out, he ordered that the image be found, but without success. When Alfonso VI arrived in Madrid, he instructed his troops and the people of Madrid to dismantle the city walls to find the image. When they reached the grain deposits, they heard a noise from the turrets above, which then collapsed, revealing an image of the Virgin and Child.

Palacio Real

The scale of the palace is undeniably awesome and the pomp is a little overwhelming. The story that sentries guarding the rear of the building used to freeze to death in the icy wind adds to the sense of chilliness it inspires.

Scaled to fit Also known as the Palacio de Oriente or the Palacio Nacional, the Royal Palace was begun under Philip V in 1737 after the old Muslim fortress was destroyed by fire in 1734. The original design by Filippo Juvanna was for facades measuring 475m (520 yards) each, or three times longer than the palace now, but there was neither the space nor the money for that. It was completed in 1764, to designs by Sacchetti. From the street side, it is a normal palatial building of the period, with Doric pilasters framing the reception hall windows. The royal family does not actually live here: it is used occasionally for state visits, during which dinner is served in the gala dining room. The entrance is to the south side of the building, across the Plaza de la Armería, which is flanked by the Royal Armoury housing El Cid's sword and suits of armour.

Interior and gardens There are more than 3,000 rooms, and most are never used. A ceiling by Conrado Giaquinto accents the grand staircase. The ceiling of the Sala de Gasparini is remarkable, done in stucco, while the ceiling of the Sala de Porcelana, built for Charles III, has a fine display of white, gold, and green porcelain plaques. To the north of the palace are the elegant Sabatini Gardens, which offer the best view of the palace, while to the rear is the Campo del Moro (Moor's Field), with a splendid Carriage Museum. The only way to see the palace is by following a fixed itinerary, which takes in the most impressive rooms.

HIGHLIGHTS

- Grand staircase
- Sala de Porcelana
- Salón de Alabarderos
- Salón de Columnas
- Sala de Gasparini
- Salón de Carlos III
- Clock collection
- Chapel by Giambattista Sacchetti and Ventura Rodríguez
- Music Museum
- Sabatini Gardens

INFORMATION

- ✚ all; C9; locator map A2
- ✉ Calle Bailén
- ☎ 91 454 88 00
- 🕐 Mon–Sat 9.30–5; Sun and public hols 9–2
- Ⓜ Opera
- 🚌 3, 25, 33, 148
- 💷 Moderate
- ↔ Catedral la Almudena (▶ 30)
- ♿ Very good

Philip II, by the Royal Palace

MADRID A FELIPE II

Plaza de Oriente

DID YOU KNOW?

- General Franco held mass rallies here
- Tunnels beneath the square date back to Moorish times
- Earliest royal with statue: King Ataulfo (AD 415)
- Statue of Philip IV is at the geometrical centre of square
- Statues brought to square in 1841
- Previous location of statue of Philip IV was Buen Retiro Palace
- Equestrian statue weighs 7,484kg (16,500 pounds)
- First performance in Royal Theatre was Donizetti's *The Favourite*

INFORMATION

✛ all; C9; locator map A2
✉ Plaza de Oriente
🍴 Café de Oriente
🎭 Opera
🚌 3, 25, 33
↔ Palacio Real (➤ 31), Monasterio de la Encarnación (➤ 33)

Have an *aperitivo* on the terrace of the Café de Oriente, with the harmonious formal gardens stretching away in front of you to the Royal Palace. This is the place to reflect on the might of the monarchy at the height of its powers.

Ambitious emperor The elegant Plaza de Oriente was planned in 1811 under Joseph Bonaparte. To build it, he had to destroy the monuments and churches that then surrounded the Royal Palace. His original aim had been to build a kind of Champs Élysées, running from the Plaza to the Cibeles Fountain. Fortunately, the Champs Élysées project was abandoned; had it not been, Madrid would have lost, among many other treasures, the Convent of the Royal Shoeless Nuns. The existing square dates from the reign of Queen Isabella II (1833–1904). The attractively laid-out gardens contain statues of the kings and queens of Spain, which were originally intended for the top of the Royal Palace facing on to the plaza, but were never put into place because they were too heavy, and Isabella II dreamed that an earthquake made them topple over onto her.

Teatro Real At the eastern end of the square stands the Royal Theatre, built between 1818 and 1850 and now restored. The open-air theatre that originally occupied the site was expanded in 1737 for a visit by Farinelli, the legendary *castrato* singer, of whom Philip V (1683–1746) was particularly fond. It reopened in 1997, after 10 years' refurbishment, on the saint's day of Queen Isabella II, its founder.

The horse The equestrian statue in the centre of the square is of Philip IV by Montañes, taken from a portrait by Velázquez.

Top: *equestrian statue of Philip IV in the plaza*

Monasterio de la Encarnación

Located away from the traffic of Calle Bailén, the Monastery of the Incarnation is the monumental equivalent of a tranquillizer, suffused with religious calm that brings peace to the soul.

History Designed by Juan Gómez de Mora in 1611 on instructions from Queen Margarita, wife of Philip III, the church in the Royal Monastery is a typical example of Habsburg Spanish religious architecture. Originally the monastery was connected by a secret passage to the Arab fortress where the Royal Palace now stands. The church was damaged by fire in 1734, and reconstructed by Ventura Rodríguez in a classical-baroque style in the 1760s; the granite facade is all that remains of the original. A 45-minute guided tour leads you through the monastery, which is still used by nuns of the Augustine order; you see the Royal Room, hung with fairly uninspired portraits of the Spanish royal family, and one of Madrid's most beautiful churches, the monastery church, which includes a reliquary. Here also is the lesser-known of Madrid's two monastery museums (the other being the Descalzas Reales, ➤ 36).

The Reliquary At the centre of the church stands an altar and altarpiece with a panel depicting the Holy Family by Bernadino Luini, a pupil of Leonardo da Vinci, and an ornate tabernacle in bronze and rock crystal. Inside is a crucifix of Christ with a crown of thorns, oddly charred: tradition holds that these are the remains of a crucifix (date unknown) that was defiled by heretics. Among the 1,500 relics on display, in a small glass globe to the right of the door as you enter, is the dried blood of St. Pantaleón, which mysteriously liquefies for 24 hours beginning at midnight every 27 July, St. Pantaleón's Day.

HIGHLIGHTS

- *John the Baptist,* Jusepe Ribera
- *Handing over of the Princesses,* anonymous painting in lobby
- *Recumbent Christ,* Perronius
- Royal Room
- Altarpiece
- Cupola, with frescoes by González Velázquez
- Frescoes: Francisco Bayeu
- Charred crucifix
- Blood of St. Pantaleón

INFORMATION

- ✛ al; C8; locator map A2
- ✉ Plaza de la Encarnación 1
- ☎ 91 454 88 00
- 🕐 Monastery and Reliquary: Tue–Thu and Sat 10.30–12.45, 4–5.45; Fri 10.30–12.45; Sun 11–1.45
- 🚇 Opera
- 🚌 3, 148
- 🎟 Inexpensive. Free Wed
- 🔁 Catedral la Almudena (➤ 30), Palacio Real (➤ 31)
- ♿ None

Plaza de la Villa

HIGHLIGHTS

- Statue of Admiral Alvaro de Bazán
- Staircase of Honour (Casa del Ayuntamiento)
- Statue of Goya (Casa del Ayuntamiento)
- Visiting Room, with engraving of oldest map of Madrid (1622) (Casa del Ayuntamiento)
- Glass patio (Casa del Ayuntamiento)
- Tapestry Room, with 15th-century pieces (Casa de Cisneros)
- Commissions Gallery

INFORMATION

- all; D9; locator map B3
- Plaza de la Villa
- 91 588 10 00
- Buildings: Mon 5–6
- Sol, Opera
- 3
- Free
- Plaza Mayor (➤ 35), Puerta del Sol (➤ 37)
- Spanish guide only for buildings. With advance phone call, guided tours in French and English can be arranged for groups
- None

With its small scale, this rectangular and typically Castilian square makes a pleasant change from some of the more imposing buildings in Madrid. Here you will see three different architectural styles in harmonious coexistence.

Casa del Ayuntamiento Dramatically floodlit at night, the plaza has been the venue for Madrid Town Council meetings since 1405. Originally the site of an Arab street market, it is now home to three buildings in three distinct styles. The Casa del Ayuntamiento, sometimes referred to as la Casa de la Villa, is Castilian-baroque. Designed in 1630 by Juan Gómez de Mora, the first to introduce rectangular forms to the Madrid landscape, it has two doors, one for the Council and one for the prison that also occupied the building. The doors you see today are baroque modifications dating from 1670. The building's facade was later altered by Juan de Villanueva in 1787, and a balcony leading on to the Plaza Mayor was added. Inside is a grand staircase and a room containing a Goya painting.

Two fine buildings The much-restored Casa de Cisneros, on the south side of the square, is one of Madrid's finest examples of the plateresque style prevalent in the 16th century. It was built as a palace by a relative of the great Cardinal Cisneros in 1537. The Torre de los Lujanes, the third noteworthy structure on the square, is one of the few monuments in Madrid surviving from the 15th century; it exemplifies the best of late Gothic civic architecture. It was the residence of one of Madrid's aristocratic families from the 1460s, and it is said that King Francis I of France was held prisoner here in 1525 by Hernando of Alarcón, who owned the house at the time.

Plaza Mayor

The cobbled Plaza Mayor strikes a chord with everyone entering it for the first time: it's here that you fully realize you are in the capital of Spain. Surely it is only in Madrid that a building as old as the Casa de la Panadería could have been frescoed over 400 years later.

Work in progress Built in the 15th century as a market square, and later renamed the Plaza del Arrabal (Square outside the Walls), the Plaza Mayor came into its own when Philip II, after making Madrid the capital of Spain, ordered it rebuilt as the administrative centre of the Court. The only part to be completed immediately was the Panadería, or the bakery, by architect Diego Sillero in 1590 (the frescoes are the work of the early 1990s), while the rest of it was completed in 1619 by architect Juan Gómez de la Mora under Philip III, whose bronze equestrian statue (by Giambologna and Pietro Tacca) stands at the centre. After a fire in 1790 much of the square had to be rebuilt. The buildings between the towers on either side of the square are Town Hall offices; the rest are private residences.

A gathering place The Plaza Mayor was where the more important members of the Court lived during the 17th century; at the end of the century, the square became the site of mounted bullfights, carnivals, and the terrible *autos da fé* of the Spanish Inquisition, attended by thousands on 30 June 1680, when 118 offenders were executed in a single day. Hangings were also carried out here until the end of the 18th century. To this day the plaza is the scene of many public gatherings.

DID YOU KNOW?

- Number of arches: 114
- Number of balconies: 377
- Shop at No. 4 opened in 1790
- Seven "Juans" have played a part in the square's history
- Three destructive fires: 1631, 1672 1790
- Philip II statue was gift from Duke of Florence
- Official name of square is Plaza de la Constitución

INFORMATION

- bII; D9; locator map B3
- Plaza Mayor
- *Terraza* bars around square
- Sol
- 3, 5, 150
- Plaza de la Villa (► 34)
- Tourist office in square

A good place to watch the world go by

Convento de las Descalzas Reales

HIGHLIGHTS

- *Recumbent Christ*, Gaspar Becerra
- *Neapolitan Nativity* (Chapel of St. Michael)
- *Virgin of the Forsaken*, Tomás Yepes
- *St. Ursula and the Eleven Thousand Virgins*, Giulio Lucini
- Bust of the *Mater Dolorosa*, José Risueño
- *Cardinal Infante Don Fernando of Austria*, Rubens
- *The Ship of the Church*, 16th-century painting
- *Adoration of the Magi*, Brueghel
- *The Empress María*, Goya
- 17th-century tapestries

INFORMATION

- bI–bII; D9; locator map C2
- Plaza de las Descalzas Reales 3
- 91 454 88 00
- Tue, Wed, Thu, Sat 10.30–12.45, 4–5.45; Fri 10.30–12.45; Sun and public hols 11–1.45
- Sol, Opera
- 3, 5, 150
- None
- Moderate. Free Wed
- Puerta del Sol (➤ 37), Real Academia de Bellas Artes (➤ 38)

Top: Recumbent Christ, by Becerra

Though the tour of the Royal Shoeless Nuns' Convent is conducted at a brisk pace, the building contains an unusually high proportion of unmissable treasures. It merits return visits.

Convent history Of Madrid's two monastery museums, the Descalzas Reales is the richer; most of its rooms are small museums in themselves. Founded by Juana of Austria, the younger daughter of Charles V, on the site of the place in which she was born, it was built between 1559 and 1564 in Madrid brick by Antonio Silla and Juan Bautista of Toledo. The church was completed in 1570 by Diego de Villanueva. The whole place breathes mid-17th-century religious mysticism, though the "vile stink"—the unpleasant smell of which traveller William Beckford complained when attending Mass here in the late 18th century—has departed. The original sisters were all of noble or aristocratic blood, and each founded a chapel on reception into the order: there are 33 of them, and to this day the convent is home to 33 Franciscan nuns, each of whom maintains one of the chapels. The Grand Staircase, with its *trompe l'oeil* portrait of Philip IV and his family standing on the balcony, is covered with frescoes by the artist Claudio Coello. With its incongruous location right in the centre of commercial Madrid, it is a small miracle that it remains intact.

The art collection The tour of the convent takes in a quarter of the rooms. Given in Spanish only, it lasts around 45 minutes and is conducted at such a frenzied pace that it is worth buying a guide book at the entrance. Unfortunately you cannot go around independently. The church can be visited only during Mass, at 8AM or 7PM.

Puerta del Sol

Almost inevitably, you will cross this square several times. For many *madrileños*, it is the true soul of the city and each year thousands gather here to see in the New Year.

Soul of Madrid The area's namesake gateway was demolished in 1570 when the square was widened to receive Anne of Austria, Philip II's fourth wife. The design of the present square dates back to 1861, the building on the south side, the Casa de Correos, is from 1768. Originally the Post Office, it is now the headquarters of the Madrid regional government. Spain's Kilometre Zero, the point from which all distances in Spain are measured, can be found on the pavement in front of it. The clock and tower were built in 1867.

A troubled history It was in Sol that the Esquilache mutiny of 1766 began, sparked by Charles III's uncharacteristically tyrannical insistence that the population should wear short capes and three-cornered hats to emulate a hated French style. The most notable moment in Sol's history was on 2 and 3 May 1808, when *madrileños* took up arms against invading French troops, a heroic resistance in which more than 2,000 died. Both days are immortalized in Goya's two magnificent anti-war paintings in the Prado, *The Second of May* and *The Third of May*. Various 20th-century uprisings also took place in Sol. It was here that politician José Canalejas was assassinated in 1912, and the Second Republic was proclaimed in 1931. It remains a popular meeting place in Madrid, especially by the monument of the bear with a strawberry tree.

HIGHLIGHTS

- Bear and *madroño* (strawberry tree) statue
- Statue of Charles III
- La Mallorquina pastry shop
- Newspaper stands: a major part of Madrid streetlife
- Tio Pepe sign
- Kilometre Zero
- Doña Manolita's lottery ticket stands

INFORMATION

- cII; D9; locator map C2
- Puerta del Sol
- Sol
- 3, 5, 15, 20, 51, 52, 150
- Plaza Mayor (➤ 35), Convento de las Descalzas Reales (➤ 36), Real Academia de Bellas Artes (➤ 38)

Statue of the bear with a strawberry tree

Real Academia de Bellas Artes

HIGHLIGHTS

- Goya self-portraits (Room 20)
- *The Burial of the Sardine*, Goya (Room 20)
- *Alonso Rodríguez*, Francisco Zurbarán (Room 6)
- *Christ Crucified*, Alonso Cano (Room 3)
- *Head of John the Baptist*, José Ribera (Room 3)
- *Felipe IV*, Velázquez (Room 11)
- *Susana and the Elders*, Rubens (Room 13)
- *Spring*, Giuseppe Arcimboldo (Room 14)
- *Martyrdom of St. Bartolome*, Ribera (Room 3)
- Goya etchings (Calcografía Nacional)

INFORMATION

- ✚ cll; D9; locator map D2
- ✉ Calle Alcalá 13
- ☎ 91 524 08 64
- 🕐 Tue–Fri 9–7; Sat, Sun, Mon, and public hols 9–2.30
- Ⓠ Sol, Sevilla
- 🚌 3, 5, 15, 20, 51, 52, 150
- 🎫 Inexpensive. Free Sat and Sun
- ↔ Convento de las Descalzas Reales (➤ 36), Puerta del Sol (➤ 37)
- ♿ Good

Though the Prado, the Thyssen, and the Reina Sofía may have more visitors, the eclectic collections of the Royal Academy of Fine Arts, the oldest permanent art institution in Madrid, are interesting to visit.

History It was Francisco Meléndez who suggested the establishment of a Royal Academy on the model of those in Rome, Paris, Florence, and other great cities. Work began on the authorization of Philip V in 1744 and was completed under Fernando VI in 1752. The Academy was initially in the Casa de la Panadería, in the Plaza Mayor, but Charles III transferred it to its present site in 1773. The original building was baroque, but shortly after it opened, Academy members with conservative tastes insisted that it be given today's neo-classical facade. Rarely overcrowded, it is small enough to be visited comfortably in a couple of hours.

Layout The museum has three floors. The best-known galleries are on the second floor, most notably Room 20 containing examples of Goya's work. Other highlights by 17th-century Spanish artists include *Head of John the Baptist* by José de Ribera (1591–1652), *Alonso Rodgriguez* by Francisco Zurbarán, and *Felipé IV* by Velázquez. Pay particular attention to the 16th-century Milanese painter Giuseppe Arcimboldo's *Spring* in Room 14—it is the only Arcimboldo in Spain and one of only a handful in the world. Half-way up the stairs to the entrance (and easily missed) is another museum, La Calcografía Nacional, or Engraving Plates Museum. The Gabinete Goya at the back of this, a hidden treasure, contains a beautifully displayed series of the original plates used by the artist for his etchings.

Colección Thyssen-Bornemisza

This is one of the best things that has happened to Madrid since the end of the Civil War. It is also one of the few internationally renowned art museums where *everything* is priority viewing.

New museum The collection was begun by the German financier and industrialist Baron Heinrich Thyssen-Bornemisza in the 1920s and continued after his death by his son, Hans Heinrich. The 755 paintings exhibited here were sold to the Spanish state for $350 million in 1993, one year after the museum opened to the public. The permanent collection, spanning seven centuries, is housed in the sympathetically remodelled 18th-century Palacio de Villahermosa. The new glass pavilion contains 19th- and 20th-century paintings from the collection of Hans Heinrich's widow, Carmen Thyssen-Bornemisza, a former Miss Spain.

The collection The sheer variety of the many works on display prompted some to call the Thyssen over-eclectic; others claim its very quirkiness is part of its charm. Each room highlights a different period; the top floor is devoted to art from medieval times through to the 17th-century, the second floor to rococo and neoclassicism of the 18th and 19th centuries through to fauvism and expressionism, the first level to 20th-century surrealism, pop art, and the avant-garde. Start from the top and work your way down. A free guide book in English is provided.

HIGHLIGHTS

- *Portrait of Giovanna Tornabuoni*, Domenico Ghirlandaio
- *Portrait of Henry VIII*, Holbein
- *St. Catherine of Alexandria*, Caravaggio
- *Annunciation Diptych*, Van Eyck
- *St. Jerome in the Wilderness*, Titian
- *The Lock*, Constable
- *Easter Morning*, Caspar David Friedrich
- *Les Vessenots*, Van Gogh
- *Man with a Clarinet*, Picasso

INFORMATION

- ✚ dII; E9; locator map E3
- ✉ Paseo del Prado 8
- ☎ 91 369 01 51
- ⏰ Tue–Sun 10–7
- 🍴 Café, restaurant
- Ⓜ Banco de España
- 🚌 1, 2, 5, 9, 10, 14, 15, 20, 27, 34, 37, 45, 51, 52, 53, 74, 146, 150
- 🚉 Atocha, Recoletos
- 💰 Moderate
- ❓ Bookstore on the lower floor
- ♿ Excellent

King Henry VIII *by Holbein*
(1497–1543)

Centro Nacional de Arte Reina Sofía

HIGHLIGHTS

- View from exterior elevators
- Enclosed patio
- *Guernica*, Picasso
- Joan Gris Room
- Picasso Room
- Joan Miró Room
- Dalí Room
- Surrealism Room
- Luis Buñuel Room
- Spanish 20th-Century Art Room

INFORMATION

- ✚ dIV; E10; locator map E4
- ✉ Calle Santa Isabel 52
- ☎ 91 467 50 62/468 30 02
- 🕐 Mon, Wed–Sat 10–9; Sun 10–2.30
- 🍴 Bar, restaurant
- 🚇 Atocha
- 🚌 6, 10, 14, 24, 26, 27, 32, 34, 36, 37, 41, 45, 47, 54, 56, 57, 85, 86
- 🚉 Atocha
- 💷 Inexpensive. Free Sat afternoon and Sun morning
- ❓ Excellent shop on first floor
- ♿ Very good

Top: *Picasso's* Guernica
Above: *external elevators on the Reina Sofia*

In Madrid's leading modern art museum, the home of Picasso's *Guernica*, you might not like all the works on display. But even on its busiest days, the light and airy space is a delight.

A triumph of planning Inspired by the Pompidou Centre in Paris, this 12,540sq-m (135,000sq-ft) space is Madrid's finest contemporary art centre; among European museums only the Pompidou is larger. It occupies a building that served as the San Carlos hospital between 1977 and 1986. Transparent lifts on the

outside whisk you up for a thrilling view over the rooftops of Madrid. The fine permanent collection showcases Spanish art of the 20th century—cubism, surrealism, realism, informalism. Most of the other spaces have temporary exhibitions; sometimes radically avant-garde.

Guernica Picasso's masterpiece dominates the Reina Sofía. When it was commissioned by the Republican Government for display at the 1937 Paris Exhibition, the only instruction was that it be big: it measures 6.4 x 7m (21 x 23ft). Taking his inspiration from the Nationalist bombing of the Basque town of Guernica in 1937, this painting has become 20th-century art's great anti-war symbol. Many saw the 1995 decision to remove the bullet-proof screen that had protected it for many years as a symbolic gesture, showing that democracy in Spain had finally taken root.

Museo Sorolla

This beautifully serene spot belonged to Spain's finest impressionist painter, Valencian Joaquín Sorolla, who wanted to create an oasis of peace for himself in a busy city. It is the best of Madrid's house museums.

Entrance and gardens The recently restored Sorolla Museum is also one of the few places in the city to give us a sense of the shape of an artist's life and work. Built in 1910–11 by Enrique María de Repollés, it was the Madrid home of Joaquín Sorolla (1863–1923) and became a museum after Sorolla's widow, Clotilde, donated it to the state. It was opened to the public in 1932. The two small gardens, designed by Sorolla himself as a setting for his collection of fountains and fonts, are a bit of Andalucía in Madrid. The first is an imitation of a part of the Seville *alcázar*, while the second is modelled on the Generalife Gardens in Granada's Alhambra. Near the entrance is a replica of a white marble bust of Sorolla by Mariano Benlliure, and to the left, opposite the entrance, is an Andalucian patio.

The house Lovingly preserved, the house is redolent with turn-of-the-20th-century elegance. The ground floor, with its salon and dining room, gives a real feeling of the artist's life; the upper floor has been converted into a gallery, each room given over to a different aspect of Sorolla's work. Be sure to visit his studio, complete with a Turkish bed, where he is reputed to have taken his daily afternoon *siesta*. Among the paintings here are several of his wife, Clotilde. Although some see a fairy-tale, picture-postcard quality in his art, there is no denying the brilliance of his handling of light—look out for the skylights, essential to capture as much light as possible while he worked.

HIGHLIGHTS

- *La Bata Rosa* (Room II)
- *Self Portrait* (Room III)
- *Clotilde en traje de noche* (Room III)
- *Clotilde en traje gris* (Room III)
- Turkish bed, used by Sorolla for *siestas* (Room III)
- *La Siesta* (Room IV)
- *Las Velas* (Room IV)
- *Nadadores* (Room V)
- *Madre* (Room VI)
- New York gouaches (Drawings Room)

INFORMATION

- E7; locator map off F1
- Paseo del General Martínez Campos
- 91 310 15 84
- Tue–Sat 10–3; Sun and public hols 10–2
- Iglesia, Rubén Darío
- 5, 7, 16, 40, 61, 147
- Inexpensive. Free Sun
- Few

41

Plaza de la Cibeles

THE SIGHTS

- Post Office
- Gardens of Palacio de Linares
- Facade of Bank of Spain building
- Post Office clock
- Robert Michel's lions
- Newspaper stand on Paseo del Prado

INFORMATION

- ✚ dl; E8; locator map E2
- ✉ Plaza de la Cibeles
- 🖳 Banco de España
- 🚌 5, 9, 10, 14, 20, 27, 34, 45, 51, 53
- 🚇 Atocha, Recoletos
- ↔ Museo del Prado (▶ 43), Palacio de Bibliotecas y Museos (▶ 45)

Despite the constant traffic, this plaza, a sheer mass of stone around a statue of the fertility goddess, La Cibeles, is Madrid's most overwhelming, the city's equivalent of the Eiffel Tower.

Cars pass by Seated imperiously at one of Madrid's busiest intersections, the goddess and her marble fountain were erected according to instructions from Charles III (1716–88). The main statue is by Francisco Gutiérrez and the lions, Hipponomes and Atlanta, drawing the goddess' chariot, are by Robert Michel. Originally at the corner of the square, the statue was finally completed in 1792 and moved under the order of the Duke of Romanones in 1895, at which date the cherubim were added.

Around the Plaza The enormous wedding-cake look-alike on the southeastern side of the square is one of Madrid's most imposing buildings. Visitors are sometimes disappointed to discover that it is only the Central Post Office—often dubbed by local wits as Our Lady of Communications. It was designed by Antonio Palacios in 1904, its painstakingly worked facade in a style reminiscent of the Viennese.

The Palacio de Linares The real treasure of the Plaza de la Cibeles is the Palacio de Linares, which is said to be haunted. It was designed in 1872 by architect Carlos Collubi, and restored and opened in 1992 as the Casa de América as a gesture of goodwill on the 500th anniversary of Columbus' discovery of America. The beautifully lit interior now showcases exhibits about Latin American visual arts. It also offers music, theatre performances and lectures. The garden is elegantly laid out, and in summer there is an excellent café-restaurant.

Top: *Central Post Office*
Above: *La Cibeles statue*

Museo del Prado

The city's pride in the magnificent Prado is justified. With its Goyas, El Grecos, and other masterpieces, it is undoubtedly one of the great art museums of the world.

Brief history Some people still believe that Madrid is a one-sight city, and that that sight is the Prado, a National Monument. The neo-classical building, completed by Juan de Villanueva in 1785, was conceived by Charles III as a centre for the study of natural sciences. After Napoleon's troops damaged it during the Spanish Wars of Succession, it was restored by Fernando VII as a home for the royal collection of paintings and sculptures and opened as a museum in November 1819. It is unequalled in the world, with a collection numbering 7,000 pictures, of which around 1,500 are on display at any given time; there are 115 Goyas, 83 works by Rubens, 50 by Velázquez, 40 Brueghels, 36 Titians, 32 El Grecos, and 20 Zurbaráns. Like all great museums, the Prado is best appreciated in more than one visit. The main entrance is the Puerta de Goya, at the northern end.

Las Meninas, Las Majas, and the "dark paintings" Do not leave the Prado without seeing Velázquez's masterpiece, *Las Meninas,* widely considered technically the finest painting in the world. Goya's *Majas*—two paintings believed to be of the Duchess of Alba, one naked, one clothed—positively beckon the spectator into the picture, Madrid's seductive answer to the Mona Lisa. Goya's *pinturas negras*—among them *Saturn Devouring One of his Sons* and *Half-Drowned Dog*—are obviously the work of a man whose sanity is in decline. At once grotesque, disturbing, and breathtaking, they are unique.

HIGHLIGHTS

- *Las Meninas,* Velázquez
- Goya's "dark paintings"
- *The 2nd of May, The 3rd of May, Las Majas,* Goya
- *The Holy Family,* Raphael
- *The Bacchanal, Emperor Charles V in Mühlberg,* Titian
- *The Garden of Delights,* Bosch
- *The Triumph of Death,* Brueghel
- *Self Portrait,* Dürer
- *David and Goliath,* Caravaggio
- *The Three Graces,* Rubens

INFORMATION

- dII–dIII; E9; locator map F3
- Paseo del Prado
- Tue–Sun 9–7; public hols 9–2
- 91 330 28 00; 90 632 22 22 (24 hours)
- Bar, restaurant, café
- Banco de España
- 1, 2, 5, 9, 10, 14, 15, 20, 27, 34, 37, 45, 51, 52, 53, 74, 146, 150
- Atocha, Recoletos
- Moderate. Free Sun
- Plaza de la Cibeles (➤ 42), Palacio de Bibliotecas y Museos (➤ 45)

Top: *Goya's* La Maja Desnuda

San Jerónimo el Real

HIGHLIGHTS

- Chapels
- 19th-century altarpiece by José Méndez
- 19th-century wooden pulpit
- Organ in choir, gift from Queen María Cristina
- Stained-glass windows
- Bronze hanging lamps

INFORMATION

- E9; locator map F3
- Calle Moreto 4
- 91 420 35 78
- Daily 10–1.30, 5–8.30; Sun and public hols 9.30–2.30, 5.30–8.30. Closed during services
- Banco de España, Retiro
- 10, 14, 19, 27, 34, 37, 45
- Atocha
- Free
- Museo del Prado (➤ 43)
- Information telephone to right of entrance
- None

This odd-looking church, a mishmash of architectural styles, has a certain solid power, and is breathtaking when you happen upon it during an evening stroll.

A royal church Also called Los Jerónimos, this Gothic church with a single nave and chapels between the buttresses has long been used by the Spanish monarchy for official ceremonies and as a spiritual retreat. Every prince of Asturias was sworn in here, from Philip II in 1528 to Isabella II in 1833. Alfonso XIII and Victoria of Battenberg were married here in 1906, and the present king, Juan Carlos I, was crowned here in 1975. Founded in 1464 by Henry IV as the San Jerónimo el Real Convent, on the banks of the Manzanares river, it was moved to its present site in 1503 and rebuilt for Ferdinand and Isabella. During the reign of Philip IV (1621–65), it was connected to the Casón del Buen Retiro, recently renovated to house the Prado's modern paintings, by underground passages. The building was badly damaged during the Napoleonic Wars in 1808; during restoration between 1848 and 1883, towers and pinnacles were added. This project did much to preserve the flavour of the original.

Cloisters When the walls of San Jerónimo's 17th-century cloisters (the oldest surviving part of the monastery) were dismantled in 2000 to make way for the expanding Prado museum, there was public uproar. However, Rafael Moneo's new gallery extension incorporates these historic remains beneath a modern glass roof. It houses temporary exhibitions and has a café, a restaurant, a lecture theatre, and conservation studios. It is linked to Juan de Villanueva's neoclassical building by a landscaped roof garden, inspired by the gardens which characterized the Paseo del Prado when it was first laid out in the 18th century.

Top: *detail from stained-glass window*

Palacio de Bibliotecas y Museos

If you are interested in the ancient roots of modern Spain, the well-lit, well-organized, and spacious National Library and Museum is fascinating to visit.

The building The huge Palacio de Bibliotecas y Museos, with its impressive neoclassical façade and eight-columned portico, was completed in 1892 to commemorate the 400th anniversary of the discovery of America, and is home to the Museo Arqueológico Nacional and the Biblioteca Nacional (National Library), founded by Philip III.

Archaeological Museum The museum is beautifully laid out, and the collection, covering prehistory up to the 19th century, is as valuable artistically as it is archaeologically. Its chief attractions, dating from the period of Spain's colonization, are the Iberian Dama de Elche and the Visigothic votive Guarrazar Crowns. The museum's entrance is at the rear of the building on Calle Serrano. Under the garden, there is a reproduction of one of the most famous and oldest cave paintings in Europe, the depiction of a herd of bison, found at Altamira.

Library On the approach to the building, there are statues of Alfonso X the Wise, Cervantes, and other historical and literary figures. Inside, the library houses 3 million volumes and 120,000 are added every year. Particularly outstanding is the 22,000-strong collection of the texts that have shaped Spanish literary history, including a 14th-century manuscript of El Cid. Although none of these books is on display, many are shown during temporary exhibitions.

HIGHLIGHTS

- Amenemhat sarcophagus (Room 13)
- Dama de Ibiza (Room 19)
- Dama de Elche (Room 20)
- Sculpture of Livia (Room 21)
- Sundial (Room 23)
- The Guarrazar Crowns (Room 29)

INFORMATION

- ✚ E8; locator map F1
- ✉ Serrano 13
- ☎ 91 577 79 12
- 🕐 Tue–Sat 9.30–8.30; Sun 9.30–2.30
- 🚇 Serrano, Colón
- 🚌 5, 14, 21, 27, 37, 45, 53
- 🚃 Recoletos
- 🎟 Inexpensive. Free Sat afternoon and Sun
- ↔ Jardines del Descubrimiento (➤ 46)
- ♿ None

Top: the Archaeological Museum
Right: the Library

Jardines del Descubrimiento

HIGHLIGHTS

- Statue of Christopher Columbus
- Tableaux set in base of statue
- Water curtain
- Inscriptions on statues
- Skateboarders
- City Cultural Centre
- Map on wall of Cultural Centre
- Botero statues

INFORMATION

- ✚ E8; locator map F1
- ✉ Plaza de Colón
- 🍴 Cafetería Restaurante del Centro Cultural
- 🎦 Colón
- 🚌 1, 5, 9, 14, 19, 21, 27, 37, 45, 51, 53, 74, 89
- 🚇 Recoletos
- ↔ Palacio de Bibliotecas y Museos (➤ 45)

Though not particularly beautiful, the Discovery Gardens exemplify recent architectural development in Madrid and put a slice of Spanish history in concrete form.

1970s Madrid Typical of Madrid town planning of the 1970s, these sculpture gardens in the Plaza de Colón were built to celebrate Spain's role in the discovery of the New World. The gardens (now being remodelled) are dominated by an 1892 Jerónimo Suñol statue of Christopher Columbus, which faces west towards the Americas—a wedding gift from the Spanish nobility to Alfonso XII (1875–85). Underneath the gardens is the Centro Cultural de la Villa de Madrid, soon to be rebuilt, offering theatre, concerts, and exhibitions, and protected from the chaos of the outside world by a deafening curtain of water. If you see it working, you may agree with those who call the fountain in the centre of the Plaza de Colón the most beautiful in Madrid.

Detail (top) on the Columbus statue (above)

The statues The Columbus statue is 17m (57ft) high, on a base with four tableaux representing scenes from the life of Columbus (Isabella offering him jewels, Columbus narrating the story of his grand project). But it is the wonderful Joaquín Vaquero Turcios sculptures from 1977 that dominate the garden. The decision to locate them so close to the more classical statues further along Paseo de la Castellana was controversial at the time. The three statues represent Columbus three ships—the *Pinta*, the *Niña*, and the *Santa María*—as they sail across the Atlantic in 1492 towards the fourth statue, which represents the New World. You can best appreciate the effect by standing well back.

Puerta de Alcalá

If you are travelling from the airport by taxi to Madrid's centre this gateway is one of the first things you will see. It is perhaps the city's most powerful emblem, particularly when lit at night.

Neoclassical symbol Listed as a National Monument, the Puerta de Alcalá is one of the great symbols of Madrid, together with Cibeles. Situated in the Plaza de la Independencia, along the line of the old city walls, it is perhaps the city's finest example of the neoclassical architecture that came as a reaction to previous baroque excesses. Commissioned by Charles III, who was to be responsible for so much of the city's architectural transformation, it was designed by Francisco Sabatini in 1778 as the main entrance to the Court. Five previous designs by other architects had been rejected.

Design Made up of five arches of granite and stone, the statue has ten columns similar to those by Michelangelo for the Capitol in Rome —facing east and crowned with Ionic capitals. Three central archways are flanked by two smaller ones. The lion heads in the centre of the three higher arches are the work of Robert Michel, and the cherubim, the trophies, and the coat of arms that surmount the statue are by Francisco Gutiérrez. You can still see the bullet-marks from the 1921 assassination attempt on Eduardo Dato, the President of Madrid's Council of Ministers, on the north side of the statue. Luckily, a recent Madrid Town Council proposal to paint parts of the *puerta* white was rejected. Best appreciated when floodlit at night, the Puerta de Alcalá stands at the centre of an immense traffic junction, so unfortunately it can be admired only from a distance.

DID YOU KNOW?

- A bullring stood near the site until 1873
- The Puerta is 22m (72ft) high (not including shield)
- Middle arches are 10m (33ft) high
- Subject of a pop song by Ana Belén

INFORMATION

- E8; locator map F2
- Plaza de la Independencia
- Retiro
- 9, 19, 15, 20, 28, 51, 52, 74
- Recoletos
- Plaza de la Cibeles (► 42)

Parque del Retiro

HIGHLIGHTS

- Palacio de Cristál
- Artichoke Fountain in the Rose Garden
- Cecilia Rodríguez Gardens
- Velázquez Palace
- Statue of Alfonso XII
- Lake
- *Fallen Angel* statue
- 400-year-old cypress tree near Philip IV entrance
- Philip IV parterre
- Observatory (1790)

INFORMATION

✚ E9–F9–F10; locator map off F2

✉ Calle Alcalá, Alfonso XII, Avenida de Menedez Pelayo, Paseo de la Reina Cristina.

🍴 *Terrazas*

🚇 Retiro, Atocha, Ibiza

🚌 2, 14, 19, 20, 26, 28, 68, 69

🚃 Atocha

↔ Colección Thyssen-Bornemisza (➤ 39), Museo del Prado (➤ 43), Puerta de Alcalá (➤ 47)

Small enough to be welcoming and undaunting, but large enough to get pleasantly lost in, the Retiro will linger in your memory, particularly if you see it in late spring or early autumn when its colours are most vivid.

History On a sunny Sunday afternoon, everyone in the city seems drawn as if by instinct to the Retiro park, 1.3sq-km (0.5sq-mi) in the city centre, whose name translates as "retreat." This is the best time to visit. Originally thickly wooded and once a hunting ground for Philip II, the Retiro was the brainchild of the Duke of Olivares, who designed it in the 1630s for Philip IV as part of the Buen Retiro Palace—a complex of royal buildings and immense formal gardens that inspired Louis XIV at Versailles. It was used until the time of Carlos III, who partially opened it to the public in the 1770s. Most of the palace was destroyed during the Napoleonic Wars.

A walk in the park Use the entrance on Calle Alfonso XII opposite the Casón del Buen Retiro. Walk through the parterre gardens and up the steps along a broad, shady avenue to the lake. If you want to take a boat out, head left around the lake; opposite you is a statue of Alfonso XII, a popular spot to soak up the sun. Otherwise, turn right and follow the lake around; just beyond where the water ends, turn left and you will come to the Palacio de Cristál (Glass Palace), the Retiro's loveliest building, constructed of iron and glass in 1886. Continuing straight ahead brings you to La Rosaleda, (the Rose Garden). From here, another left turn takes you to the statue of the *Fallen Angel* (the Devil), a right turn to the Cecilia Rodríguez Gardens. A left turn at the end of the gardens will bring you to the Velázquez Palace, which hosts art exhibitions.

Museo Lázaro Galdiano

There cannot be many museums like this wonderful oddity, which is surprisingly unfamiliar to many *madrileños*. Every time you go, there is something new and eye-catching to discover in this dazzling collection.

A noble art collector José Lázaro Galdiano, an obsessive, seemingly unfocused art collector who died in 1948 at the age of 80, was born into Navarre nobility. He married Paola Florido, an Argentinian who shared his affinity for art, and together they devoted their lives to travelling the world in search of treasures. An essentially private man, Galdiano never revealed how much he paid for any of the masterpieces. On his death, he donated his collection to the state, and the museum opened its doors to the public in 1951. Now completely reorganized, the exhibition begins on the ground floor with an assessment of Lázaro's role as patron and collector and displays a representative sample of the collection, which includes paintings by Hieronymus Bosch, Bartolomé Murillo, Rembrandt, Francisco Zurbarán, El Greco, Velázquez, José de Ribera, Turner, and Goya, as well as exquisite gold and silverwork, enamelwork, bronzes, medieval stained glass, jewellery, fans, rock crystal, and weaponry.

Parque Florido The collection is housed in the Parque Florido, a neo-Renaissance *palazzo* named after Lázaro's wife. The beautifully restored interiors provide a magnificent setting for the treasures on exhibition and are one of many treats in store for visitors. Don't miss the spectacular painted ceilings, commissioned specially by Lázaro to decorate what were orginally the family's private apartments. This is the finest of Madrid's smaller art galleries.

HIGHLIGHTS

- *The Virgin of Charity*, Caravaggio
- *Landscape*, Gainsborough
- *Saint John in Patmos*, Bosch
- *Portrait of Saskia van Uylendorch*, Rembrandt
- *Luis de Góngora*, Velázquez
- *The Adoration of the Magi*, El Greco

INFORMATION

- ✚ F6; locator map off F1
- ✉ Serrano 122
- ☎ 91 561 60 84
- 🕐 Wed–Mon 10–4.30
- 🚇 Nuñez de Balboa/Rubén Dario
- 🚌 12, 16, 19, 51, 89
- 💶 Inexpensive
- ♿ None

Top: The Adoration of the Magi *by El Greco*
Below: *the Parque Florido Palace*

Plaza de Toros

- Holds 22,000 people
- A papal bull in the museum (1567) bans bullfighting
- *Portrait of Joaquín de Rodrigo*, attributed to Goya
- First fights held here in 1931
- A "suit of lights" may contain 5kg (11 pounds) of gold embroidery

INFORMATION

- H7; locator map off F1
- Avenida de los Toreros, Calle Alcalá 237
- 91 725 18 57
- Museo Taurino: Tue–Fri 9.30–2.30; Sun 10–1
- Ventas
- 12, 21, 38, 106, 110, 146.
- Museo Taurino free
- Best visited in May during Feria de San Isidro
- None

Bullfight poster

Is bullfighting art or blood sport? No matter what your feelings, you cannot help but be impressed by the world's most important bullring, the place in which a bullfighter must triumph if he is to achieve international recognition.

History and architecture Officially opened in 1934, this is also Madrid's finest example of neo-Mudéjar architecture, a style that resurfaced during the 19th century in imitation of the Mudéjar architecture of the 13th and 14th centuries and is defined by an interesting use of brickwork and attractive, bright ceramic tile inlay. In the square in front of the bullring is a melodramatically posed statue in memory of bullfighter José Cubero, inscribed with the deathless words "a bullfighter died, and an angel was born."

Museo Taurino Half an hour in the stuffy Museo Taurino next to the stables gives you a basic overview of the famous names in bullfighting, if not of the complex art of bullfighting itself. Massive heads of legendary bulls and portraits of great bullfighters line the walls, and there are several dramatic portrayals of bull-runs, including a notable one by artist and sculptor Mariano Benlliure (1868–1947). The highlights are the *trajes de luce* (suits of lights), as they are known, among them one belonging to Juanita Cruz, an early 20th-century woman bullfighter who was never allowed to fight on Spanish soil, and another worn by Manolete, who was perhaps the greatest of them all when he died in the ring in 1947. The museum displays are labelled both in Spanish and English, unusual in Madrid's museums.

MADRID's
best

Museums & Galleries

SOME TIPS

Museo in Spanish is not the same as "museum" in English, but means both "museum" and "non-commercial art gallery"—thus the "Museo del Prado." Madrid has many, some unknown even to locals. Some are run by the state and others privately; the latter generally have better facilities and staff, although very few have facilities for non-Spanish speakers.

CASA MUSEO LOPE DE VEGA

Spain's greatest playwright, Felix Lope de Vega (1562–1635), lived in this house from 1610 until his death. Now an evocative museum, the rooms are furnished in the style of the period, based on an inventory by Lope himself. The highlights include the chapel (he was also a priest), the book-lined study, the embroidery room—the wall-hangings kept out the cold—and the garden.

➕ E9 ✉ Calle de Cervantes 11 ☎ 91 429 92 16 🕐 Tue–Sat 11–2, 5–8; Sun, public hols 11–2 🚇 Banco de España 🚌 on Paseo del Prado 💷 Inexpensive (short guided tour, Spanish only)

Fresco in the Casón del Buen Retiro

CASÓN DEL BUEN RETIRO

This was originally the ballroom of the Buen Retiro Royal Palace, a building destroyed by Napoleonic troops but then rebuilt by Charles III, who instructed Luca Giordano to decorate the vault with frescoes. Today it contains the Prado's 19th-century Spanish art collection. A Prado ticket gets you in.

➕ E9 ✉ Calle Alfonso XII 68 ☎ 91 420 05 68/420 06 70 🕐 Tue–Sat 9–7; Sun 9–2 🍴 Restaurant 🚇 Retiro 🚌 19 💷 Inexpensive; free on Sat and Sun afternoon ♿ Very good

FUNDACÍON JUAN MARCH

One of Europe's most important private art foundations, this is home to around 30 major annual exhibitions. Often among the most interesting to be found in Madrid, these have focused on Picasso, Kandinsky, and Matisse. The permanent collection is largely made up of contemporary Spanish art.

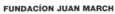

➕ F7 ✉ Calle Castelló 77/Calle Padilla 36 ☎ 91 435 42 40 🕐 Mon–Sat 10–2, 5.30–9; Sun and public hols 10–2. Closed Aug and between exhibitions 🚇 Nuñez de Balboa 🚌 29, 52 💷 Free ♿ Very good

MUSEO DE LA CIUDAD

Opened in 1992, this spacious four-storey Museum of the City is a high-tech equivalent of the Museo Municipal, and at every step there is the odd sense of seeing Madrid repeating itself in miniature. The museum explains in almost numbing detail the workings of Madrid's roads and rail, telephone, and water systems, and there are some attractive scale models and lots of interactive displays. There are often good temporary exhibitions.

🏛 F6 ✉ Calle Principe de Vergara 140 ☎ 91 588 65 99 🕐 Tue–Fri 10–2,4–7; Sat–Sun 10–2 🚇 Cruz del Rayo 🚌 29, 52 💷 Free ❓ Guided tours can be arranged in advance ♿ Excellent

MUSEO MUNICIPAL

The Municipal Museum, built between 1721 and 1729 on the site of an old hospice, traces the history of Madrid through archaeological discoveries, paintings, and maps; some lovely landscape paintings show an older, greener city; and there are works by Francisco Bayeu, Vincente Carducho, and Goya—a dramatic allegory of Madrid among others—as well as a striking model of the city constructed in 1830. The fine baroque doorway was designed by Pedro Ribera, the outstanding architect of Madrid's Golden Age.

www.munimadrid.es 🏛 D8 ✉ Calle Fuencarral 78 ☎ 91 588 86 72 🕐 Tue–Fri 9–9; Sat–Sun 9–2; Aug 9.30–2.30. Closed public hols 🚇 Tribunal 🚌 149 💷 Inexpensive; free on Wed and Sun ♿ None

MUSEO ROMÁNTICO

This monument to faded romantic glory, founded in 1924, finally undergoing a much-needed restoration, is inside a typical mid-18th-century *madrileño* building that was the home of the traveller-painter the Marqués de Véga-Inclán. Though the content—primarily 18th-century art—might be too sentimental for some tastes, there are many items of interest, particularly Alenza's miniature *Satires of Romantic Suicide*, Goya's *Saint Gregory the Great*, and a collection of Isabelline and Imperial furniture.

🏛 E8 ✉ Calle San Mateo 13 ☎ 91 448 10 71 🕐 Tue–Sat 9.30–3; Sun and public hols 10–3. Closed Aug 🚇 Tribunal 🚌 21, 37 💷 Inexpensive; free on Sunday ♿ Very good

MUSEO DEL TRAJE

The brand new Museum of Costume draws on more than 21,000 items of clothing—everything from shoes to mantillas—to illustrate the historical evolution of Spanish dress from the Middle Ages to the 20th century. Experts believe that the museum's star exhibit, the 13th-century trousseau of the Infanta María, daughter of Ferdinand III, is the oldest civil costume of its kind.

🏛 B6 ✉ Avenida Juan de Herrera 2 ☎ 91 549 71 50 🕐 Mon–Sat 9.30–7; Sun and public hols 10–3 🚇 Moncloa, Ciudad Universitaria 🚌 14, 27, 40, 147, 150 💷 Moderate ♿ Good

CLOSURES

It is unlikely that all the sections of all the museums in Madrid have ever been open simultaneously. Redecoration and renovation—necessary evils—can be frustrating, especially since any enquiry about reopening time is likely to be met by a shrug of the shoulders. Many museums are closed on Monday.

Outside the Casón del Buen Retiro

Plazas

PLACES OF CELEBRATION

Whether round or oblong, the plaza, or square, is central to a Spaniard's conception of his environment. The plazas have always been focal points where the community gathers, particularly to celebrate; they still have that function today. Check at metro stations for advertisements of events due to take place in a nearby plaza. Even when you do not understand what is going on, the lively atmosphere will reward your efforts.

Crowds gather in the city's plazas as religious processions pass by

---

In the Top 25

17 PLAZA DE LA CIBELES (► 42)
9 PLAZA DE LA VILLA (► 34)
7 PLAZA DE ORIENTE (► 32)
10 PLAZA MAYOR (► 35)
12 PUERTA DEL SOL (► 37)

PLAZA DE CASCORRO

In the heart of the *barrio popular* of old Madrid, this plaza is at the top end of the fabled Rastro street market, named after the traces of blood left by animals on their way to the slaughterhouse that once stood nearby—*Rastro* means "stain." It is a perfect place to experience the hustle and bustle of the Old Quarter on a late Sunday morning. On the right stands Los Caracoles, a long-established seafood bar that is typical of the area. Just down Calle Ribera de Curtidores, there is a statue of local hero Eloy Gonzalo, while at the top of Calle Embajadores there is an immense mural depicting the Rastro as it was one hundred years ago.
➕ bIII; D9 ✉ Plaza de Cascorro 🚇 La Latina, Tirso de Molina 🚌 17, 23, 35

PLAZA DE LA CEBADA

This is one of the more authentic squares even though it no longer looks like a square. Its market, opened 1875, was Madrid's first example of iron architecture; before its erection, bullfights were held on the site, and at the beginning of the 19th century, it was the scene of public executions (► 55, panel).
➕ bIII; D9 ✉ Plaza de Cascorro 🚇 La Latina, Tirso de Molina 🚌 17, 23, 35

PLAZA DE LAS CORTES

This is the home of the Congreso de los Diputados, or parliament buildings. The ceremonial entrance to the parliament is guarded by two bronze lions popularly known as Daoíz and Velarde after the heroic captains of the Napoleonic invasion, cast from cannons brought back from the African War in 1860. An attempted military *coup* took place inside the building in 1981, and was recorded on video for posterity. There are weekly guided tours.
➕ dIII; E9 ✉ Plaza de las Cortes 🚇 Sevilla 🚌 5, 150, N5, N6

PLAZA DE ESPAÑA

A statue of Cervantes stands at the western end of this grandiose, slightly daunting square, overlooking a rather lovable 1815 statue of his two legendary creations, Don Quixote and Sancho Panza. On the edge of the square with a neo-baroque doorway is the

Edificio España, Madrid's first true skyscraper, while the 137m (450ft) Torre Madrid was a symbol of post-Civil War economic recovery and was Europe's tallest building when it was built in 1957.

🚩 C8 ✉ Plaza de España 🚇 Plaza de España 🚌 68, 69, 74, 133

PLAZA DE LA LEALTAD

A stone's throw from the Prado, this elegant, semicircular plaza dominated by the Ritz Hotel has an obelisk at the centre to the memory of those who died at the hands of Napoleonic troops on 3 May 1808. Their ashes are kept in an urn at the base of the monument. The Madrid Stock Exchange was built here in 1884, in a neoclassical design that neatly echoes the Prado.

🚩 dII; E9 ✉ Plaza de la Lealtad 🚇 Banco de España 🚌 10, 14, 27, 34, 37, 45

PLAZA DOS DE MAYO

This is the heart of the historic *barrio* of Malasaña, once slightly run-down and disreputable, but now cleaned up with a children's play area and some inviting outdoor cafés. The eponymous Manuela Malasaña and her daughter became heroes when helping to defend the area from attack during the invasion of Napoleonic troops on 2 May 1808. In the square, there is a statue of the two captains who led the resistance, Daoíz and Velarde.

🚩 D8 ✉ Plaza 2 de Mayo 🚇 Bilbao 🚌 21, 147

PLAZA DE LA PAJA

During Muslim rule, this pleasant little Straw Square was the site of the city's most important *zoco*, or street market; during the Middle Ages, it housed aristocratic residences. Of the many palaces located here, the most notable is at No. 14, the Lasso de Castilla, the preferred residence of Catholic kings when they stayed in Madrid, sadly, now extremely unpalatial in appearance.

🚩 aIII; C9–D9 ✉ Plaza de la Paja 🚇 La Latina 🚌 3, 31, 148

PLAZA DE SANTA ANA

Once occupied by the Santa Ana monastery, which was torn down during Joseph Bonaparte's rule (1808–13), the recently refurbished plaza is now surrounded by bars and is perfect for people-watching in summer. A statue of playwright Calderón de la Barca stands in the centre, and the Teatro Español was built in 1849 at the eastern end after the original building, an open-air theatre, was gutted by fire.

🚩 cII; D9 ✉ Plaza de Santa Ana 🚇 Sol, Sevilla 🚌 5, 150

The statue of Cervantes in the Plaza de España

EXECUTIONS IN THE PLAZA DE LA CEBADA

Public executions took place in Madrid until early in the 20th century. The instrument of death was the particularly nasty *garrote vil*, which was screwed around the neck and tightened. Most famous among the many criminals executed in the Plaza de la Cebada was Luis Candelas, the popular bandit, who was put to death in 1837.

Churches

THE BELL OF SAN PEDRO EL VIEJO

"St. Peter's the Elder" is so called to distinguish it from another St. Peter's in Madrid of more recent construction. According to legend, the original bell was so large that it could not be taken up to the bell tower, and was left leaning against the walls overnight. The following morning it had mysteriously raised itself into the tower. The miracle led to the belief that the bell had magical powers, such as the ability to ward off thunderstorms. The bell was removed in 1565.

CONVENTO DE SAN ANTÓN

Designed by Pedro Ribera and built by Juan de Villanueva, this example of baroque architecture houses a magnificent art collection, highlighted by Goya's *The Last Communion of Saint José de Calasanz*, painted between 1775 and 1780, and architect Ventura Rodríguez's *Dolphins* statue.
🔂 E8 ✉ Hortaleza 63 ☎ 91 521 74 73 🚇 Tribunal, Chueca

SAN ANDRÉS

The undoubted highlight of this National Monument is the Capilla del Obispo (Bishop's Chapel, currently closed for restoration) built between 1520 and 1530 and reflecting the transition between the Gothic and Renaissance periods. The nave and apse have Gothic vaulted ceilings, while the decorative aspects are Renaissance. The fine wooden altarpiece was carved by Francisco Giralta, the paintings above it by Villoldo el Mozo. The dome over the sanctuary of the San Andrés Chapel is late 15th century.
🔂 alll; C/D9 ✉ Plaza de San Andrés 1 ☎ 91 365 48 71
🕐 Mon–Sat 8–12.30, 6–8, Sun 9–2; do not visit during Mass. Closed public hols 🚇 La Latina, Tirso de Molina 🚌 3, 148 ♿ None

SAN FRANCISCO EL GRANDE

Built between 1761 and 1784, this church has a neo-classical facade by Francisco Sabatini, one of the greatest practitioners of this style, and an overwhelming 33m (108ft) dome by Miguel Fernández. The monastery was used as a barracks from 1835, after which it was lavishly redecorated. The interior (note the ceiling frescoes) contains much work by Spanish masters, including an early Goya, *The Sermon of San Bernadino de Siena*, in the first chapel on the left. There is also a museum.
🔂 alll; C9 ✉ Plaza de San Francisco ☎ 91 365 38 00 🕐 Tue–Sat 11–1, 5–7 🚇 La Latina, Tirso de Molina 🚌 3, 7, 60, 148 ♿ None

Santa Bárbara, in Calle Bárbara de Braganza

SAN ISIDRO

San Isidro is the patron saint of Madrid, and between 1885 and 1993, until the completion of the Almudena, this immense baroque church was

Madrid's unofficial cathedral. Built in 1620 by Pedro Sánchez for the Jesuits, the church was commandeered by Charles III after he expelled them. San Isidro's remains, until then in San Andrés, were brought here at that time. There is a festival in his name in May (➤ 4).

✚ bIII; D9 ✉ Calle Toledo 37–39 ☎ 91 369 20 37 🚇 La Latina 🚌 17, 23, 35 ♿ None

The basilica of San Francisco el Grande

SAN NICOLÁS DE LOS SERVITAS

This is Madrid's oldest church, and though much restored after the Civil War, its tower is one of the very few echoes of the Arabic Madrid in the city. Designated a National Monument, the tower is probably the minaret of a mosque later consecrated as a Catholic church. This 12th-century tower is Mudéjar (built by Muslims under Christian rule), while the central apse is Gothic. Juan de Herrera, employed by Philip II as the architect of El Escorial, was buried in the crypt in 1597.

✚ aII; C9 ✉ Plaza de San Nicolás 6 ☎ 91 559 40 64 🕓 Mon 8.30–2; Sun 10–2, 6.30–8.30; do not visit during Mass. Not always open; advance phone call advisable 🚇 Opera, Sol ♿ None

SAN PEDRO EL VIEJO

Noteworthy principally for its 14th-century Mudéjar tower and the legends surrounding it (➤ 56, panel), San Pedro stands on the site of an old mosque. In the doorway are the only coats of arms extant from the period preceding the Catholic monarchs. Part of the interior dates from the 15th century, while the rest is largely of 18th-century construction.

✚ aIII–bIII; D9 ✉ Calle Nuncio 14 ☎ 91 365 12 84 🕓 Daily 6–8PM; do not visit during Mass 🚇 La Latina, Tirso de Molina ♿ None

SANTA BÁRBARA (LAS SALESAS REALES)

Probably the grandest, if not the most attractive, of Madrid's churches, Las Salesas was commissioned by Bárbara de Braganza, the wife of Fernando VI. It has an elaborate facade built between 1750 and 1758 by Carlier and Moradillo, and contains Sabatini's tomb of Fernando VI (1713–59). The adjoining monastery is currently the home of the Palacio de Justicia, or Supreme Court.

✚ E8 ✉ Calle Bárbara de Braganza 3 ☎ 91 742 19 21 🕓 Daily 5–7PM; do not visit during Mass 🚇 Alonso Martínez, Colón

VISITING CHURCHES

When visiting churches, dress formally, wear long trousers or skirts of a decorous length rather than shorts, and cover your shoulders. Photos should be taken without flash, and if there is a service in progress, simply stand at the back and observe in silence. Some churches do not like visits during Mass, unless for religious purposes.

Monuments & Statues

MADRID'S GATEWAYS

The *puertas*, or gateways, of Madrid, are one of its distinguishing features. Each of them was built to mark the end of one of the principal routes into the city. The Puerto de Toledo, the gateway to the city from the royal road from Andalucia, was begun by Joseph Bonaparte in 1813 and completed in 1827. It was to be the last of Madrid's gateways. They are at their best at night, when they are illuminated.

BOTERO STATUES

In 1994, a section of Castellana was devoted to an exhibition of sculptures by 20th-century sculptor, Fernando Botero. When the exhibition ended, *madrileños* retained a *Hand* in the middle of Castellana; the *Reclining Woman* in Calle Génova; and *Man on a Mule* in the Plaza de Colón.

➕ E8; E6 ✉ Colón, Plaza de San Juan de la Cruz 🚇 Colón, Nuevos Ministerios 🚌 7, 14, 27, 40, 147, 150

FALLEN ANGEL (PARQUE DEL RETIRO)

The fallen angel in question is Lucifer: *madrileños* tell you that this is the world's only statue created in his honour. It is by Ricardo Bellver and dates from 1881.

➕ F9 ✉ Retiro, Glorieta del Angel Caido 🚇 Atocha 🚌 19, 20

FUENTE DE LOS DELFINOS

Housed in the San Antón convent on Calle Hortaleza, the *Dolphins* statue is the work of Ventura Rodríguez.

➕ E8 ✉ Calle Hortaleza 63 ☎ 91 521 74 73 🚇 Tribunal, Chueca 🚌 3, 7 ♿ None

FUENTE DE LA FAMA

The Ribera Gardens are now a playground behind the Municipal Museum; the pretty baroque fountain (Fountain of Fame) by Pedro Ribera remains a delight.

➕ D8 ✉ Jardines del Arquitecto Ribera, Calle Barceló 🚇 Tribunal 🚌 21, 37, 40, 48

FUENTE DE NEPTUNO

In the Plaza de Cánovas de Castillo, the Neptune fountain by the 18th-century sculptor Ventura Rodríguez shows the King of the Sea riding a carriage in the shape of a shell, pulled by two horses.

➕ dII; E9 ✉ Plaza de Cánovas del Castillo 🚇 Banco de España 🚌 10, 14, 27, 34, 37, 45

MUSEO DEL ARTE CONTEMPORÁNEO AL AIRE LIBRE

Connecting the Calles Juan Bravo and Eduardo Dato is a walkway over the Paseo de la Castellana. Underneath is an open-air display of sculpture by many of Spain's best-known contemporary artists.

➕ E7–F7 ✉ Paseo de la Castellana 🚇 Rubén Dario 🚌 5, 14, 27, 37, 45

Botero's Hand *in the Castellana*

Parks & Green Spaces

In the Top 25

2 PARQUE DEL OESTE (▶ 27)
23 PARQUE DEL RETIRO (▶ 48)

CASA DE CAMPO

In Casa de Campo (▶ panel), you can walk for a couple of hours without being interrupted (best avoided after dark). The park contains sports facilities, a large lake, and the Parque de Atracciones (▶ 60), with more than 40 amusement park rides from gentle merry-go-rounds to the stomach-churning Top Spin. A *teleférico* (cable car) runs up to the Parque del Oeste (▶ 27), considered one of the city's most delightful green spaces.

➕ B8–B9 ✉ Calle Marqués de Monistrol, Avenida de Portugal 🚇 Lago, Batán 🚌 41, 33, 39, 65, 75, 84

FUENTE DEL BERRO

This intricate little 17th-century garden, just south of the bullring and unfortunately close to the M30 motorway, is a well-kept secret. The attractive Berro fountain is surrounded by lush greenery. There is plenty of welcome shade in summer and several eye-catching statues.

➕ H8 ✉ Alcalde Sainz de Baranda 🚇 O'Donnell 🚌 15

JARDÍN BOTÁNICO

These peaceful gardens are the result of overseas expeditions in search of interesting species dating back to the 18th century. The plants and trees are carefully classified and laid out along geometrical walkways.

➕ E9 ✉ Plaza de Murillo 2 🚇 Atocha 🚌 10, 14, 27, 34, 37, 45

JARDINES DE LAS VISTILLAS

The best place in Madrid for sunset-watching, this park has wonderful views over the Casa de Campo towards the Guadarrama Mountains. From late spring to autumn it's also a lively place to go in the evening for a drink.

➕ C9 ✉ Travesía Vistillas 🚇 Opera, La Latina 🚌 3, 148

LOS CAPRICHOS DE ALAMEDA DE OSUNA

This is the closest Madrid comes to a formal English garden. Though a fair distance from the centre, it is pleasant for Sunday strolls.

➕ Off map ✉ Paseo de la Alameda de Osuna 🚇 Canillejas

A GREEN CITY

That Madrid is one of Europe's greenest capital is mainly because of the 1,722 ha (4,256-acre) Casa de Campo, "the lungs of Madrid," stretching away to the northwest. Once a royal hunting estate, it was opened to the public in 1931. Boats can be rented and it is considered one of the city's most attractive open spaces, a cool haven in Madrid's hot summer.

View of the city from Casa de Campo

59

Attractions for Children

In the Top 25

🅿 PARQUE DEL OESTE (➤ 27)
🅿 PARQUE DEL RETIRO (➤ 48)

TREN DE LA FRESA

Hostesses in costume serve strawberries to passengers on this old steam train, which is called the Strawberry Train because it runs between Madrid and the Aranjuez strawberry fields. A hundred years ago, the trip was a favourite weekend jaunt for *madrileños*. Tickets can be reserved by many travel agents, and include entrance to the Royal Palace and gardens in Aranjuez.

AQUÓPOLIS

Spanish children beg their parents to take them to Aquópolis, the biggest and best of the Madrid water parks and one of the largest in Europe. There are huge water slides, an adventure lake, and wave machines.

🚫 Off map ✉ Villanueva de la Cañada. Carretera de El Escorial 25km ☎ 91 815 69 33 🕐 Mid-Jun to Sep noon–8PM (11PM weekends) 🍴 Cafés

FAUNIA

Europe's only theme park dedicated to nature and biodiversity. The eight pavilions, each of which re-creates a different ecosystem with the authentic sights, sounds, smells, flora, and fauna, will amaze and delight. Experience a tropical rain storm and find out what it's like to live among polar bears in the Arctic.

🚫 Off map ✉ Avenida de las Comunidades 28 ☎ 91 301 62 10 🕐 Summer: Mon–Fri 10.30–8, Sat, Sun 10.30–9; winter: Wed–Sun 10–6 🍴 Cafés 🚇 Valdebernado 💰 Expensive

PARQUE DE ATRACCIONES (CASA DE CAMPO)

There are open-air concerts in summer at this amusement park with everything from merry-go-rounds to the breathtaking Tornado roller-coaster.

🚫 A9 ✉ Casa de Campo ☎ 91 463 29 00 🕐 Mon–Fri noon–1AM; Sat and public hols noon–2AM 🍴 Cafés, restaurants 🚇 Batán 🚌 33, 36, 39, 65 💰 Moderate

WARNERBROS PARK

This huge theme park on the outskirts of Madrid opened in 2003. Each of the five zones has a theme: Cartoon Village, Hollywood Boulevard, the Wild West, Super Heroes, and Warner Studios.

🚫 Off map ✉ San Martin de La Vega. NIV to km22, then M-506 and follow signs ☎ 91 821 1234 🕐 Apr–Jun, Sep, Mon–Thu 10–8, Fri–Sun 10–midnight; Jul, Aug daily 10–midnight; Oct to mid-Nov, Fri–Sun 10–8 🍴 Cafés, restaurants 🚇 C3 from Atocha 💰 Expensive

ZOO

Madrid's zoo is one of the best in Europe. It contains over 2,000 animals and more than 100 species of bird, including 29 endangered species. There is a dolphinarium with twice-daily shows, a train ride, an aquarium, and a children's section. Parrot shows, the tank of sharks, and birds of prey are all popular.

🚫 A9 ✉ Casa de Campo ☎ 91 512 37 70 🕐 Daily 10.30–dusk 🍴 Cafés, restaurants 🚇 Batán 🚌 33, Ventas–Zoo, Batán–Zoo, Estrecho–Zoo, Peñaprieta–Zoo 💰 Expensive

The dolphinarium—a perennial attraction at the zoo in the Casa de Campo

Interesting Streets

ARENAL

Connecting Sol with Opera, the Calle Arenal has a 19th-century air. During the Middle Ages, it was no more than a ravine, but after 1656, it began to compete with the Calle Mayor in importance, perhaps because it was the shortest route between the Royal Palace and Sol. Highlights are the San Ginés Church and the Joy Eslava discotheque.
✛ bII ◷ 9 🚇 Sol, Opera 🚌 5, 15, 20, 51, 52, 53, 150

GRAN VÍA

Running between the Calle Alcalá and the Plaza de España, the imposingly massive Gran Vía is one of the city's great axes; with its shops and cinemas, it is very lively and stimulating for early evening strolls. Begun in 1910 under Alfonso XII, it led to the shortening or destruction of 54 other streets. Highlights are the Grassy jewellers (corner of Calle Alcalá) and the skyscraper Telefónica buildings.
✛ bI–cI, D–E8 🚇 Gran Vía, Callao 🚌 44, 46, 74, 133, 146, 147, 148, 149

MAYOR

This is perhaps the most traditional of Madrid's streets, with some fusty, old-fashioned shops—including a wonderful *guitarrería* (guitar store) near the Calle Bailén end. Spain's two greatest playwrights, Lope de Vega and Calderón de la Barca, lived at Nos. 25 and 61 respectively.
✛ aII–bII; D9 🚇 Sol 🚌 3

MESÓN DE PAREDES

To get a complete sense of the slightly surreal and multicultural atmosphere of Madrid's *barrio popular*, stroll down this street and those around it on any weekday morning when it is bustling and full of life. La Corrala is an 1882 example of the corridor-tenement found throughout working-class Madrid. Beginning in the early 1980s it was used for productions as an open-air theatre. It is now an Artistic Monument.
✛ bIII–cIII–cIV; D9–D10 🚇 Tirso de Molina, Lavapies 🚌 32, 57

PASEO DE LA CASTELLANA

Running in an almost straight line from Colón for 6.5km (4 miles) to Plaza de Castilla, the Castellana is one of Madrid's main points of reference and a centre of business and nightlife. It splits the city in two, and many major sights are on or around it.
✛ E2–E8 🚇 Colón, Rubén Darío, Nuevos Ministerios, Lima, Cuzco, Plaza de Castilla 🚌 5, 14, 27, 40, 45, 147, 149, 150

STREETS AND SKY

Madrileños live on the streets, particularly in summer, so any description of any one of them is also a portrait of the people who work and live there. Look for the old ladies selling lottery tickets lined up on their seats in the Plaza del Sol, the waiters in the Plaza Mayor, and the market traders in the Retiro. Remember to look up, too: on clear days, the contrast between the buildings and the blue sky is exhilarating.

The Gran Vía, one of Madrid's major streets

Curiosities

MURALLA ARABE

What little we can see of the Arab Wall is the oldest surviving part of Madrid. It was originally part of the walls of the small Arab town of Magerit. The area around it, now the Parque Emir Mohammed I, is one of the venues for Madrid's autumn arts festival (➤ 4).

✚ all; C9 ☒ Cuesta de la Vega 🚇 Opera 🚌 3, 41, 148

ESTACIÓN DE ATOCHA

Some 2,000sq m (21,520sq ft) of indoor tropical garden can be found inside this impressive late 19th-century

wrought-iron station canopy by Alberto del Palacio.

✚ dIV; E10 ☒ Plaza del Emperador Carlos V ☎ 91 527 31 60 🚇 Atocha 🚌 14, 27, 34, 37, 45 ♿ Few

CASA DE LAS SIETE CHIMENEAS

Legend has it that Philip II built the House of the Seven Chimneys in the 1580s for one of his mistresses, who is said to haunt the house. During restoration, the skeleton of a woman was discovered with coins nearby from the period of Philip II.

✚ dl; E8 ☒ Plaza del Rey 🚇 Banco de España 🚌 1, 2, 74, 146

Facade of the Atocha Railway Station

CURIOUS FACTS

Behind its walls Tirso de Molina metro station has skeletons, discovered when the station was built in the 1920s. They proved to be bones from the Convent of the Merced, which previously stood on this site. Also curious is that Madrid has not been particularly careful about the remains of some of its greatest artists: the whereabouts of Velázquez, Lope de Vega, and Cervantes are unknown, while the skeleton of Goya is headless.

SALA DEL CANAL DE ISABEL II

Considered one of Madrid's finest examples of industrial architecture, this display space, built in neo-Mudéjar style between 1907 and 1911, mounts frequent excellent photographic exhibitions.

✚ D6 ☒ Calle Santa Engracia 125 ☎ 91 445 10 00 🕐 Tue–Sat 10–2, 5–9; Sun and public hols 10–2 🚇 Cuatro Caminos 🚌 3, 37, 149 💷 Free

TORRES KIO (PUERTA DE EUROPA)

These towers are named after the Kuwaiti Investment Office, which withdrew funding halfway through construction. The walls are angled inwards at 15 degrees—more than that and they would collapse.

✚ E3 ☒ Plaza de Castilla 🚇 Plaza de Castilla 🚌 5, 27, 42, 124, 125, 147, 149

VIADUCT

Known as "the Suicide Bridge" until the city council put up suicide-proof screens in 1997. Unfortunately these detract from the drama of the views down on the Calle de Segovia far below.

✚ C9 ☒ Calle Bailén 🚇 Opera 🚌 3, 148

MADRID
where to...

Madrileño Cuisine

PRICES

For dinner per person with wine, expect to pay approximately:
€ = €10–25
€€ = €25–45
€€€= €45–75

MADRID GASTRONOMY

In Madrid cuisine, the animal parts that tend to produce a grimace of disgust elsewhere play a major part: you'll find the spicy *callos a la madrileña* (offal), *orejas* (pig's ears), *sesos* (brains), and different kinds of *morcilla* (blood sausage). Perhaps the most acceptable dish to non-native palates is the classic *cocido completo*: first a noodle soup, then a main course with meat, chick peas, and other vegetables, all cooked together.

BOTÍN (€€)

Botín first opened its doors in 1725, making it, according to the *Guinness Book of Records*, the world's oldest restaurant. Suckling pig, roasted in a wood-fired oven, is the Castillian special dish.
🔆 bIII; D9 ✉ Calle Cuchilleros 17 ☎ 91 366 42 17 🚇 La Latina

CAFÉ DE ORIENTE (€€)

Built on the remains of a convent and facing the Royal Palace, this is a rather aristocratic place with distinctive dishes that fuse *madrileño* with French cuisine.
🔆 aII; D9 ✉ Plaza de Oriente 2 ☎ 91 547 39 74 🚇 Ópera

CASA ALBERTO (€)

Characterful restaurant, founded in 1827, at the back of a bar that serves terrific *tapas*. It's full of bull-fighting memorabilia. The ham croquettes and oxtail are recommended.
🔆 cIII; D9 ✉ Calle Huertas 18 ☎ 91 429 93 56 🚫 Closed Sun night, Mon and 2 weeks in Aug 🚇 Antón Martín

CASA DOMINGO (€)

Callos (tripe) is the special dish in this noisy 1920s restaurant, with outdoor tables opposite the Parque del Retiro. *Tortilla de bacalao* (cod tortilla) is another unusual speciality. Wonderful desserts.
🔆 F8 ✉ Calle Alcalá 99 ☎ 91 431 18 95 🚇 Retiro

CASA LUCIO (€€€)

The King has been known to bring visitors to this Madrid classic. The least touristy of Madrid's traditional restaurants, Casa Lucio specializes in Castilian roasts, but offers several Basque dishes in addition. A cheaper option is to order the very tasty *tapas* at Casa Lucio's bar.
🔆 aIII; D9 ✉ Cava Baja 35 ☎ 91 365 32 52 🚫 Closed Sun lunch Aug 🚇 La Latina, Tirso de Molina

LAS CUEVAS DE LUIS CANDELAS (€€)

Named after a 19th-century bandit who hid in the cellars under Plaza Mayor, this busy restaurant serves hearty helpings of roast meat and *cocido madrileño* (stew).
🔆 bIII; D9 ✉ Calle Cuchilleros 1 ☎ 91 366 54 28 🚇 La Latina

LOS GALAYOS (€€)

The best restaurant close to the Plaza Mayor, serving traditional roasts. Has open-air dining.
🔆 bII; D9 ✉ Calle Botaneras 5 ☎ 91 366 30 28 🚇 Sol

LA GRAN TASCA (€€€)

Famed for its rich and heavy but delicious *cocido madrileño*. Business clientele at lunch, more laid-back at dinner.
🔆 E7 ✉ Santa Engracia 161 ☎ 91 534 46 34 🚫 Mon–Sat. Closed Sun, and Mon night 🚇 Alonso Martínez

VIUDA DE VACAS (€)

Madrileños like to bring overseas visitors here for traditional Spanish cooking amid *azulejo* tiles and wooden tables.
🔆 bIII; D9 ✉ Calle Cava Alta 23 ☎ 91 366 58 47 🚫 Closed Sun night Aug 🚇 La Latina

Basque & Catalan Cuisine

ASADOR FRONTON (€€€)

You could easily miss this first-floor restaurant (entrance in Calle Jesús y Maria) which serves some of the best charcoal-grilled fish and steaks in the city.

➕ b–clll ✉ Plaza de Tirso de Molina 7 ☎ 91 369 23 25 🚇 Tirso de Molina

CARMENCITA (€)

This pleasant, relaxed bistro in a central location is one of the city's lower-priced Basque restaurants. Also offers *madrileño* cuisine.

➕ dl; E8 ✉ Calle Libertad 16 ☎ 91 531 66 12 🕐 Mon–Fri, Sat dinner only 🚇 Banco de España

DANTXARI (€€ €€€)

This Basque tavern has spicy cod, lamb with garlic and wild mushrooms. Wide-ranging Spanish wine list, cheerful service.

➕ C8 ✉ Ventura Rodriguez 8 ☎ 91 542 35 24 🕐 Lunch, dinner. Closed Sun dinner 🚇 Plaza España

ENDAVANT (€€)

Spacious, with a Mediterranean air and Catalan-based cuisine including snails and a delicious *crema catalana* (custard). Outdoor dining in summer.

➕ F6 ✉ Calle Velázquez 160 ☎ 91 561 27 38 🚇 República Argentina

ERROTA–ZAR (€€)

Basque-style grilled meat and fish are the house specials here. In a side room you can help yourself to *txiri* Basque wine in elegant but informal surroundings. Centrally located.

➕ dll; D9 ✉ Calle Jovellanos 3 ☎ 91 531 25 64 🚇 Sevilla

LA FONDA (€€)

One of the first Catalan restaurants in the city, offering cuisine with a creative touch, in the city's most exclusive shopping district.

➕ F8 ✉ Calle Lagasca 11 ☎ 91 577 79 24 🚇 Retiro

GOIZEKO KABI (€€€)

In a strong field, this Basque restaurant stands out for its simple but highly inventive cooking. The *bacalao a la vizcaína* (cod, Bizkaia-style) is out of this world.

➕ E5 ✉ Comandante Zorita 37 ☎ 91 533 02 14 🚇 Alvarado

OTER EPICURE (€€€)

Among the Basque and Navarre offerings, the salted fish is excellent. You can sample any of 175 wines and try any of the many cigars before you buy.

➕ F7 ✉ Calle Claudio Coello 71 ☎ 91 431 67 71 🕐 Mon–Sat 🚇 Nuñez de Balboa

ZALACAÍN (€€€)

Once considered one of Madrid's best and most expensive restaurants. Head chef, Benjamin Urdaín's Basque/Navarre menu changes seasonally .

➕ E6 ✉ Alvarez de Baena 4 ☎ 91 561 59 35 🕐 Closed Sun lunch, Christmas and Easter week 🚇 Rubén Dario

REGIONAL CUISINE

Spanish regional cuisine—particularly that of the Basque country—has achieved greater international recognition than the cuisine of Madrid itself. Basque and Catalan cuisine tends to be fish-based, though if you do order meat, it is likely to come in the form of a huge steak. Basque *tapas* are available at some of the Basque restaurants; these are little culinary works of art.

Galician & Asturian Cuisine

REGIONAL FARE

After the Basques, the Galicians have the best cuisine in Spain. Together with their neighbours the Asturians, they prefer maritime cuisine, and the portions are generally sizeable with potatoes the staple food. Regional special dishes include *pulpo* (squid), and *pimentos de Padrón* (hot green peppers)—generally best eaten with a jug of water.

A'CASIÑA (€€)

The Columnas, just one of the restaurant's large dining areas, is a sunlit indoor terrace overlooking the park. Start with *arroz caldoso con bogavante*, a rich lobster soup cooked with rice and follow up with the hake (*merluza*). Reservations are essential.
✚ B9 ✉ Avenida de Angel, Casa de Campo ☎ 91 526 34 25 Ⓖ Closed Sun night Ⓜ Lago

CASA D'A TROYA (€€)

Many *madrileños* rate this as Madrid's best Galician restaurant. Its virtues are simplicity, homeliness, and first-class cooking. Try the *pulpo a feira* (octopus steamed with olive oil and paprika) with a bottle of Ribeiro or one of the other local wines.
✚ H5 ✉ Emiliano Barral 14 ☎ 91 416 44 55 Ⓖ Closed Sun Ⓜ Avenida la Paz

CASA GALLEGA (€)

The specials are largely Galician and fish-based but you'll also find fabulous Padrón peppers, as well as wonderful *tapas* in the basement bar. Service is friendly, if slow.
✚ bII; D9 ✉ Plaza de San Miguel 8 ☎ 91 547 30 55 Ⓜ Sol

CASA PARRONDO (€€)

Traditional Asturian cuisine and the steaming platefuls of tasty *fabada* (white bean and meat stew) are made with ingredients from the family's own garden.
✚ bII; D8 ✉ Calle Trujillos 4 ☎ 91 522 62 34 Ⓖ Closed Aug Ⓜ Santo Domingo

COMBARRO (€€€)

Mouth-watering seafood brought in daily from Galicia. The buzzing ground-floor *tapas* bar is one of Madrid's most attractively laid-out.
✚ D5 ✉ Calle Reina Mercedes 12 ☎ 91 554 77 84 Ⓖ Mon–Sat and Sun lunch. Closed Aug Ⓜ Alvarado

EL ESCARPÍN (€€)

This lively *taberna* showcases food from the Asturias region of northern Spain. Local specialities include *fabada* (a nourishing bean soup) and *chorizo* (spicy sausage) traditionally cooked in cider, the Asturian farmers favourite beverage.
✚ D9 ✉ Calle de las Hileras 17 ☎ 91 559 99 57 Ⓜ Sol

O'PAZO (€€€)

The king of Galician cuisine in Madrid, Don Evaristo García Gómez, serves marvellous Galician fare—seafood cocktail, Aguinaga eels, and a classic *tarta de Santiago* for dessert.
✚ E5 ✉ Calle Reina Mercedes 20 ☎ 91 553 23 33 Ⓖ Closed Sun, Easter week, and Aug Ⓜ Estrecho

LA TRAINERA (€€€)

Unarguably the best place in Madrid if you're a fan of seafood and fresh fish (*jamon iberico* is the only meat course on the menu). The distinguished wine list is especially strong on Galician varieties.
✚ cIII ✉ Calle Lagasca 60 ☎ 91 576 80 35 Ⓖ Closed Sun Ⓜ Serrano

Latin-American Cuisine

LA CABAÑA (€€–€€€)

Spaniards look to Argentinians when it comes to rustling up a good steak. This busy restaurant, near Sol, is in great demand so advanced reservations are essential, especially at weekends.
🔲 E9 ⬚ Ventura de la Vega 10 ☎ 91 420 17 41 ⬚ Lunch, dinner ⬚ Sevilla

EL CENTRO CUBANO (€)

The Cuban Centre is as much a cultural project as a restaurant: walls are covered with newspaper clippings and photos of Cuban stars past and present. Go for *ropa vieja* (meat stew) and *arroz a la cubana* (rice with tomato sauce and a banana).
🔲 F8 ⬚ Calle Claudio Coello 41 ☎ 91 575 82 79 ⬚ Serrano

EL CHALET (€€)

Summer is the best time to visit this spot with extensive pine-shaded lawns. One area is for families; the other is more intimate. Argentinian beef is the special dish.
🔲 H4 ⬚ Calle Arturo Soria 207 ☎ 91 415 64 00 ⬚ Closed Sun night ⬚ Arturo Soria

ENTRE SUSPIRO Y SUSPIRO (€€)

The best Mexican restaurant in Madrid. Very colourful, with a menu in verse. Reserve ahead.
🔲 bII; D9 ⬚ Calle Caños del Peral 3 ☎ 91 542 06 44 ⬚ Mon–Sat. Closed Aug ⬚ Opera

TAQUERÍA DE BIRRA (€)

An atmospheric Mexican spot. Try the *enchiladas* or the *acos del pastor*, prepared in the traditional way and don't miss the wonderful margaritas.
🔲 D8 ⬚ Plaza de las Comendadoras 2 ☎ 91 522 80 49 ⬚ Closed Aug ⬚ Noviciado

LA TAQUERÍA DEL ALAMILLO (€)

Mexican restaurant where the spices aren't modified to accommodate Spanish tastes. Eye-catching surroundings with hand-woven rugs and Diego Ribera paintings. Desserts include papaya ice-cream and crêpes.
🔲 aIII; D9 ⬚ Plaza del Alamillo ☎ 91 364 20 88 ⬚ La Latina

LA VACA ARGENTINA (€€)

In this successful Spanish restaurant chain, meat arrives vacuum-packed daily from Argentina. It's then served raw for you to cook to your own taste on red-hot plates.
🔲 aIII; D9 ⬚ Calle Bailén 20 ☎ 91 365 66 54 ⬚ La Latina

ZARA (€€)

Just off the Gran Vía, this small, very busy restaurant began life as a meeting place for expatriate Cubans. No frills Caribbean cooking with typical dishes such as *ropa vieja* (stewed meat in tomato sauce, served with rice and beans).
🔲 cI; E8 ⬚ Infantas 5 ☎ 91 532 20 74 ⬚ Closed Sat, Sun and Aug ⬚ Gran Via

NEW TASTES

For historical and geographical reasons, both Latin American and North African cuisine are increasingly popular on Madrid's hitherto fairly conservative culinary scene. The menus can be as incomprehensible to Spaniards as to any visitor. The best bet is to see what others are eating and order what looks appealing.

National & International Cuisine

TIPS FOR DINING

Many of Madrid's better restaurants are more enjoyable in the evenings than at lunchtime, when they attract a mainly business clientele. Only Zalacaín (► 65) insists on a jacket and tie. Only in pricier restaurants is there a chance that the waiter will speak English. Restaurants are generally open until midnight and so serve food until 10.30–11. There is no protocol about tipping: leave 5–10 percent of the bill if you feel the meal and service deserved it. Some of the best restaurants are in the best hotels (► 86): Berceo-Le Divellec in the Hotel Villa Magna (☎ 91 587 12 34; Belagua in the Santo Mauro (☎ 91 369 69 00).

ARTEMISA (€)

The best of a very few vegetarian restaurants. Green beans in a pine-nut and mayonnaise sauce is a special dish. Good value.
✚ cll; E9 ⊠ Ventura de la Vega 4 ☎ 91 429 50 92 🚇 Sol

LA BROCHE (€€€)

The newest member of Madrid's culinary elite, Chef Sergi Arola has already earned two coveted Michelin stars for his artful interpretation of traditional Catalan dishes such as *turbot con patas de puerco* (stew made with turbot and pig's feet).
✚ E7 ⊠ Calle Miguel Angel 29 ☎ 91 399 34 37 🕐 Closed Sat and Sun 🚇 Gregorio Marañon

CABO MAYOR (€€€)

This relaxed Madrid classic in elegant nautical style specializes in the cuisine of northern Spain. The lobster salad and the desserts are very good.
✚ F4 ⊠ Calle Juan Ramón Jiménez 37 ☎ 91 350 87 76 🕐 Closed Easter week and Aug 🚇 Plaza de Castilla, Cuzco

CAFE SAIGON (€€)

Reservations are essential for this hip Vietnamese restaurant. One draw is the decoration—lattice wood-carving, hessian, sepia photographs—which re-creates a bygone era. Opt for the Vietnamese dishes if you like spicy food or there's a reasonably priced *menú del degustación*.
✚ F6 ⊠ Calle Maria de Molina 66 (corner of Paseo de Castellana) ☎ 91 563 15 66 🚇 Gregorio Marañon

CANDELA (€€€)

This favourite with politicians and luminaries from the entertainment world serves huge chunks of Argentinian meat. Spacious and elegant.
✚ E5 ⊠ Calle Santo Domingo de Silos 6 ☎ 91 562 79 42 🚇 Santiago Bernabeu

LOS CUATRO ESTACIONES (€€–€€€)

Traditional cuisine with a creative twist. As the name, Four Seasons, suggests, the menu changes through the year depending on what's freshest in the markets.
✚ D6 ⊠ Calle General Ibañez de ibero 5 ☎ 91 553 63 05 🚇 Guzmán el Bueno

DIVINA LA COCINA (€€)

Fashionable Chueca restaurant which has made waves with its creative fusion cooking. Try the marinated tuna, with pistachios and herbs, or *bacalau* (cod), perked up with ginger and soy sauce.
✚ dl; E8 ⊠ Calle Colmenares 13 ☎ 91 531 37 65 🚇 Banco de España

GULA GULA (€)

A good self-service salad bar and a nightly cabaret (in Spanish) make the meal memorable. There is a smaller and less frenetic branch in Calle Infante.
✚ cll; E8 ⊠ Gran Via 1 ☎ 91 522 87 64 🚇 Sevilla

HORCHER (€€€)

Perhaps the best-known restaurant in Madrid after Zalacaín (► 65). Established in 1943 with an exquisite menu of central European dishes and game.

⊞ E9 ✉ Calle Alfonso XII 6 ☎ 91 522 07 31 Ⓒ Closed Aug Ⓜ Retiro

HYLOGUI (€)

Enormous, bustling, and one of the better basic Spanish food eateries, with more than 100 items on the menu and better-than-average service.

⊞ cII; E9 ✉ Calle Ventura de la Vega 3 ☎ 91 429 73 57 Ⓒ Closed Aug Ⓜ Sevilla

JOCKEY (€€€)

Madrid's highest prices don't deter the loyal clientele here. The menu includes fish, wild fowl, and game and changes according to the season. Try lobster *ragout* with truffles and fresh pasta or the lamb *à la provençale*.

⊞ E8 ✉ Calle Amador de los Rios 6 ☎ 91 319 24 35 Ⓜ Colon

MI PUEBLO (€€)

This small restaurant has a loyal clientele attracted by the cosy ambience and traditional home cooking (*cocina casera*). It is one of only a few places serving a local wine—from Arganda del Rey south of the city.

⊞ aII; D9 ✉ Costanilla de Santiago 2 ☎ 91 548 20 73 Ⓒ Closed Sun night, Mon Ⓜ Opera

PEDRO LARUMBE (€€€)

This has acquired classic status for the creativity of its Mediterranean cuisine. Three salons occupy the fourth floor of a beautiful neo-classical building. Summertime *terraza*.

⊞ F7 ✉ Calle de Serrano 61

☎ 91 575 11 22 Ⓒ Closed Sat lunch, Sun, 2 weeks in Aug Ⓜ Rubén Dario

SALVADOR (€–€€)

Everyone from intellectuals to bullfighters are welcome here, in the spirit of one of its long-ago regulars, Ernest Hemingway. Traditional food, with good oxtail and cod fritters.

⊞ dI; E8 ✉ Calle Barbieri 12 ☎ 91 521 45 24 Ⓒ Closed Aug Ⓜ Chueca, Gran Via

SAMARKANDA (€)

Attractive restaurant in the tropical garden section of the Atocha railway station with light, modern, international cuisine. Ask for table No. 20.

⊞ E10 ✉ Glorieta de Carlos V, Atocha Railroad Station ☎ 91 530 97 46 Ⓜ Atocha

TABERNA DE ANTONIO SÁNCHEZ (€)

The best-conserved of all the *tapas* bars pays homage to the bullfighting family that has run it since 1830. Displays on bullfighting (including bulls' heads) make the distinctive setting as fascinating as the *tapas*.

⊞ bIII; D9 ✉ Calle Mesón de Paredes 13 ☎ 91 539 78 26 Ⓜ Tirso de Molina

VIRIDIANA (€€€)

Hung with stills from Buñuel movies. The menu of superior modern Spanish food is extremely creative. The atmosphere is unusually mellow.

⊞ dII; E9 ✉ Calle Juan de Mena 14 ☎ 91 523 44 78 Ⓒ Closed Aug Ⓜ Retiro

BUDGET EATING

Many restaurants offer a *menu del dia* (often hidden away at the back of the menu) that includes a first and second course, wine and a dessert or coffee. It is not a bad idea to eat early (around 1.30–2) if you want this menu as the best items may have gone by the time you arrive. *Paella* on Thursday, for example, is always in demand. In a budget restaurant, you should be able to find a good meal for under €25, including wine.

Coffee, Tea & Chocolate

LA TERTULIA

Until not so long ago, a *tertulia* (literary gathering) was a common sight in Madrid. Writers, philosophers, and artists would meet to drink coffee (and stronger brews, too), to smoke, and to debate ideas, to such an extent that poet and musician Emilio Cerrère was inspired to declare that most literary masterpieces were written in cafés. The *tertulia* also gave rise to another phenomenon: the so-called *naufragos del café* (coffee shipwrecks), men who went to *tertulias* only to become lost in a world of unrealizable dreams. Nowadays the tradition has moved to TV, and has a new name—the talk show.

CAFÉ CIRCULO DE BELLAS ARTES

Visit one of the art exhibitions here, then enjoy coffee or a light lunch in this delightful art deco salon. Summer terrace overlooking Calle de Alcalá. Nominal entrance fee.

➕ dll; E9 ✉ Marques de Casa Riera 2 ☎ 91 360 54 00 Ⓜ Banco de España

CAFÉ COMERCIAL

"Time hasn't actually stopped in this café," declared the newspaper *El País*, "but it does move imperceptibly slowly." The Comercial, calm by day but hectic at night, is Madrid's best-known meeting point.

➕ D7 ✉ Glorieta de Bilbao 7 ☎ 91 521 56 55 Ⓒ Closed Aug Ⓜ Bilbao

CAFÉ DE NUNCIO

This friendly place in the currently trendy La Latina quarter really comes to life in summer when the *terraza* opens on the steps leading to the historic church of San Pedro El Viejo.

➕ alll; C9 ✉ Nuncio 12/Segovia 9 ☎ 91 366 08 53 Ⓜ La Latina

CAFÉ DE ORIENTE

One of the more exclusive cafés with sumptuous decor and a good view of the Palacio Real.

➕ all; C9 ✉ Plaza de Oriente 2 ☎ 91 541 39 74 Ⓜ Opera

CAFÉ GIJÓN

Best known for its literary associations, but still a pleasant place to stop.

➕ dl; E8 ✉ Paseo de Recoletos 21 ☎ 91 521 54 25 Ⓜ Banco de España, Colón

CAFÉ ISADORA

The décor in this stylish cocktail bar pays tribute to the famous American dancer, Isadora Duncan. Snacks are available as well as unusual liqueur coffees. A good place to enjoy a quiet drink in busy Malasaña.

➕ D8 ✉ Calle Divino Pastor 14 ☎ 91 445 71 54 Ⓒ 4PM–2AM Ⓜ Bilbao

CHOCOLATERÍA SAN GINÉS

Flashy, big, and extremely busy, especially in winter. Three minutes from Sol.

➕ bll; D9 ✉ Pasaje de San Ginés 5 ☎ 91 365 65 46 Ⓜ Sol, Opera

EMBASSY

The best of Madrid's few tearooms serves a wide range of teas as well as chocolates, cakes, sandwiches, and scones.

➕ E8 ✉ Paseo de la Castellana 12 ☎ 91 576 00 80 Ⓜ Colón

EL ESPEJO

With its fabulous art-nouveau decor and a terrace, El Espejo looks more expensive than it is.

➕ dl; E8 ✉ Paseo de Recoletos 31 ☎ 91 308 23 47 Ⓜ Colón

SALON DEL PRADO

A good hideaway where the *tapas* can be recommended, also the live classical music (Thu until 10.30PM).

➕ c/dll ✉ Calle del Prado 4 ☎ 91 429 33 61 Ⓜ Antón Martín

Tapas

EL ANCIANO REY DE LOS VINOS
Particularly famous for its wines, this is one of the more historic taverns of Madrid, with its *azulejo* tiles. Typical Madrid *tapas* are available, including fried cod, tripe, and meatballs.

➕ cll; D9 ✉ Calle de la Paz ☎ 91 559 53 32 ⏰ Closed Aug 🚇 Sol

LA ARDOSA
The artist Goya once drank in a bar on this site, hence the Goya prints which line the walls of this tiny, atmospheric *taberna*. There's an imaginative selection of *tapas* and *raciones* available, and Guinness and Pilsner Urqell are on draught. Tables are harder to come by.

➕ D8 ✉ Calle Colón 13 ☎ 91 521 49 79 🚇 Tribunal

CASA LABRA
The Spanish Socialist Party was founded here in 1879 just 19 years after the bar was established, and Casa Labra has been producing typically *madrileño tapas* ever since. Cod croquettes are a house special.

➕ cll; D9 ✉ Calle Tetuán 12 ☎ 91 532 14 05 🚇 Sol

CASA MINGO
A popular Asturian *sidrería* or cider house. The idea is to pour the cider into the glass from a great height and drink it very fast. The best *tapas* are based on the strong *Cabrales* cheese. The restaurant is excellent.

➕ B8 ✉ Paseo de la Florida 34 ☎ 91 547 79 18 🚇 Norte

ESTAY
This modern café in the heart of the Salamanca shopping district serves an excellent range of hot and cold *tapas*, as well as mouth-watering desserts such as mango mousse and apple compote with French toast.

➕ E8 ✉ Hermosilla 46 ☎ 91 578 04 70 🚇 Serrano

JOSÉ LUIS
Firmly non-traditional, José Luis offers *tapas* such as smoked salmon tartare and melted Brie.

➕ F7 ✉ Calle de Serrano 89 ☎ 91 563 09 58 🚇 Serrano

LAS LETRAS
Small restaurant near Plaza Santa Ana which casts new light on traditional regional dishes. (Who would have thought that black pudding, for example, could have the creamy texture of a paté?) Also featuring are tasty salads, soups, and dishes of the day.

➕ cll ✉ Calle Echegaray 26 ☎ 91 429 48 43 🚇 Sol

LHARDY
One of the city's classier restaurants and a local institution. The good range of fairly pricey *tapas* downstairs includes consommé, croquettes, Russian salad on bread, and, in summer, Madrid's best gazpacho. There is also a delicatessen.

➕ cll; D9 ✉ Calle Carrera de San Jerónimo 8 ☎ 91 521 33 85 🚇 Sol

TAPAS

The *tapa*, a snack to accompany your drink, is a part of Spanish culture: It started in the 18th century when Carlos III insisted that his entourage cover their wine with a plate of food to keep dust from getting into it (*tapa* means "lid"). Free *tapas* are largely a thing of the past, and many bars no longer display their wares, which can make it hard to order. It may be worth eating in places where the *tapas* are kept behind glass, so you can see them before buying. Pay for what you have eaten and drunk before leaving, rather than on a round-by-round basis. Many *cervecerías* (late-night bars) sell *tapas* and make an atmospheric venue for a late-night snack (➤ 82).

Markets & Shopping Streets

THE MUNICIPAL FOOD MARKETS

There are many of these around Madrid and each *barrio* has its own. All offer a vast range of foodstuffs at extremely competitive prices—and are therefore loaded with atmosphere—there are shoppers in these places who would kill to save a few cents on a clove of garlic. Especially worth visiting: San Miguel ✉ Plaza de San Miguel, is right in the centre of town; Maravillas ✉ Bravo Murillo 122, is the biggest; and Chamartín ✉ Calle Potosi, is the most elegantly laid out.

CALLE ALMIRANTE

During the 1980s, the Calle Almirante became one of the trendiest streets in Madrid. Although it has lost its edge a little, it is still the best Madrid has to offer away from the far less daring formality of Ortega y Gasset and Serrano.
➕ E8 ✉ Calle Almirante 🚇 Chueca

CALLE JOSÉ ORTEGA Y GASSET

Now Madrid's most exclusive street, with Adolfo Domínguez, Kenzo, and Giorgio Armani stores.
➕ F7–G7 ✉ Calle José Ortega y Gasset 🚇 Rubén Darío, Nuñez de Balboa

CALLE DE LOS LIBREROS

A second home for Madrid's bibliophiles for over a century. A wide range of second-hand books is available with particular emphasis on the academic.
➕ bI; D8 🚇 Santo Domingo

CALLE FUENCARRAL

This apparently unexceptional street is worth investigating for its original and offbeat shops and boutiques. Outstanding are the party fashions at No. 47 and the silver jewellery at La Reserva (No. 64).
➕ cI ✉ Calle Fuencarral 🚇 Tribunal

CALLE PRECIADOS

This pedestrianized street runs between the Plaza del Sol and the Gran Vía, and contains FNAC (books, CDs, electrical goods), and El Corte Inglés. Its central location and keen prices make it very crowded at Christmas.
➕ bI–dI; D8–D9 🚇 Sol

CALLE DE SERRANO

You will find Adolfo Domínguez, Loewe, Purificación García (► 74), and a number of household names.
➕ F7; F8 ✉ Calle de Serrano 🚇 Serrano

CONDE DE BARAJAS MARKET

Painters try to sell their latest masterpieces in this pretty little square behind Plaza Mayor.
➕ bI; D9 ✉ Plaza del Conde de Barajas 🕐 Sunday morning 🚇 La Latina

RASTRO STREET MARKET

On Sunday mornings, around 10.30 to 3, the streets around Ribera de Curtidores are thronged with people buying and selling just about everything. A lot of the wares, particularly in the side streets, are junk, but the people-watching is great. Calle Ribera de Curtidores has furniture, antiques, and camping shops.
➕ bIII–bIV; D9–D10 ✉ Plaza de Cascorro, Calle Ribera and sidestreets 🕐 Sun & public hols 🚇 La Latina, Tirso de Molina

STAMPS AND COINS MARKET

People meet to discuss stamps and coins under the archways of the Plaza Mayor.
➕ bII; D9 ✉ Plaza Mayor 🕐 Sunday morning 🚇 Sol

Key Shops & Malls

ABC SERRANO
Set in a building that once housed the ABC newspaper, this elegant mall on five levels has gifts, crafts, and fashion together with restaurants and cafés. Top Madrid is an attractive rooftop bar in summer.
🏢 F7 ✉ Calle de Serrano 61 ☎ 91 577 50 31 🚇 Rubén Dario

CENTRO COMERCIAL MADRID-2, LA VAGUADA
Madrid's largest and brashest shopping mall, with over 350 stores. One floor has a cinema, discotheque, and bars.
🏢 D2 ✉ Monforte de Lemos 36 ☎ 91 730 10 00 🚇 Barrio del Pilar

EL CORTE INGLÉS
These department stores dominate Spanish retail. They are so vast, it is almost absurd, and you can buy just about anything. Services are available as well as goods and there's also a well-stocked supermarket. Information desks are staffed by multi-lingual assistants. There are 19 branches in and around Madrid.
🏢 F8 ✉ Calle Goya 76 (with branches at Calle Preciados 3; Calle Princesa 42; Raimundo Fernández Villaverde 79) ☎ 91 418 88 00 🚇 Goya

EL JARDÍN DE SERRANO
A small, elegant cluster of fashion and accessory shops in the heart of Madrid's fashionable *barrio Salamanca*. Its cafés are the perfect place to recharge your energies for more shopping.
🏢 F8 ✉ Calle Goya 6–8 ☎ 91 577 00 12 🚇 Serrano

FNAC
Five floors of books and CDs, plus a small concert area where you can occasionally hear big names. Also has Spanish and foreign newspapers, photograph developing services, and a ticket agency.
🏢 bI; D8 ✉ Calle Preciados 28 ☎ 91 595 61 00 🚇 Callao

NEWSPAPER KIOSK IN PUERTA DEL SOL
This is the only one of the city's hundreds of bright, cheerful kiosks that is open 24 hours a day. It sells not only foreign newspapers and a startling range of pornography, but also academic studies of Nietzsche and Kant.
🏢 bII; D9 ✉ Puerta del Sol 🚇 Sol

VIPS
The 12 bright, bold VIPS stores around the city, convenient and impressive in size, sell books, magazines, and CDs, along with food and gifts. Most are open 24 hours. Each also has a bar and restaurant.
🏢 bI; D8 ✉ Gran Via 43 (with branches throughout the city) ☎ 91 559 66 21 🚇 Callao

SHOPPING AROUND
For better or worse, the retail scene in Madrid is increasingly dominated by chain stores and *centros comerciales* (shopping malls). Try and get into the back streets, to visit smaller establishments, and join the queue. Shop assistants can be sloth-like when it comes to serving customers they don't know, and "service with a smile" is only now starting to catch on. Larger stores are open through lunch, while smaller ones continue, in time-honoured fashion, to close from about 1.30 to about 4.30.

Trendsetters

NEW MADRID FASHION

Though not yet Paris, Rome, London, or even Barcelona, Madrid is slowly gaining a foothold in the world of men's and women's fashion. The international success of Adolfo Domínguez has been followed by that of Roberto Verino, and together with the avant-garde designs of Agatha Ruiz de la Prada and Jesús del Pozo, the Spanish designers are proving a serious threat to more established Italians. The *beau monde* does much of its shopping in the *barrio Salamanca*.

ADOLFO DOMÍNGUEZ

The work of Spain's best-known fashion designer is characterized by its beautiful, classic cut and its subdued colours. A men's shop is close by, at Calle Ortega y Gasset 4.
🞥 F6 ✉ Calle de Serrano 18 and 96 ☎ 91 577 82 80 🚇 Rubén Darío

AGATHA RUIZ DE LA PRADA

Agatha's daring, brightly coloured patchwork designs still fly the flag for the *movida*, that era in the mid-1980s when Madrid believed everything was there just to be enjoyed. Drinks are served every Thursday at 8PM; stop by to see what is happening.
🞥 E7 ✉ Calle Marques de Riscal 8 ☎ 91 310 44 83 🚇 Rubén Darío

ANGEL SCHLESSER

Top Spanish designer Angel Schlesser specializes in prêt-à-porter women's clothes and accessories. His signature touches include low-key colours and sober, but stylish lines.
🞥 F7 ✉ Calle Claudio Coello 46 ☎ 91 435 48 69 🚇 Serrano

ARMANI

The sobriety and elegance of this shop provides the best possible showcase for the clothes. An Emporio Armani is at Claudio Coello 77.
🞥 F7 ✉ Ortega y Gasset 16 ☎ 91 576 10 36 🚇 Nuñez de Balboa

L'HABILLEUR

The pick of last season's designer fashions at reductions of up to half price is reason enough to make a beeline for this clothes shopper's paradise. The problem is tearing yourself away.
🞥 cl; E8 ✉ Plaza de Chueca 8 ☎ 91 531 32 22 🚇 Chueca

LOEWE

This international Spanish design firm is best known for its leather bags and fashion accessories.
🞥 E8 ✉ Calle de Serrano 26 and 34 ☎ 91 577 60 56 🚇 Serrano

MITSUOKO

If you're looking for sleek leisurewear for young professionals, head for this spacious and relaxed shop to browse through the array of international labels.
🞥 d ✉ Calle Fuencarral 59 ☎ 91 523 73 85 🚇 Chueca

PURIFICACIÓN GARCÍA

The sleek look, one of the trademarks of this distinguished Spanish designer of prêt-à-porter men's and women's clothing, is reflected in the minimalist layout of the store.
🞥 E8 ✉ Calle de Serrano 28 and 92 ☎ 91 435 80 13/576 72 76 🚇 Serrano

ZARA

Now a household name around the world, Spanish designer Zara has five high street stores in Madrid, offering stylish mainstream fashion for men and women at down-to-earth prices.
🞥 bl; D8 ✉ Gran Via 32 ☎ 91 522 97 27 🚇 Gran Via

Antiques & Gifts

ANTIGUA CASA TALAVERA

Every inch of this wonderful old shop is stacked with traditional Spanish ceramics—you'll find shapes and designs from all over the country, all handmade and decorated in regional patterns.

✛ bI ✉ Calle Isabel la Católica 2 ☎ 91 547 34 17 Ⓜ Santo Domingo

BARRIO SALAMANCA

This area has over 50 antiques shops—nine in Calle Claudio Coello, six in Nuñez de Balboa, and four in Calle Velázquez. Particularly noteworthy are Sant-Yago (Calle Hermosilla 37), specializing in glassware; the Mercadillo Balboa (Nuñez de Balboa 63), a collection of auction houses under one roof that sell as well as auction; Rodriguez (Claudio Coello 85); and La Trastienda de Alcalá (Calle Alcalá 64), specializing in quality reproductions.

✛ F8 ✉ Barrio Salamanca Ⓜ Serrano, Velázquez, Nuñez de Balboa, Claudio Coello

CÁNTARO

A treasure-trove of Spanish ceramics, with everything from traditional pieces to modern tableware.

✛ bI ✉ Calle Flor Baja 8 ☎ 91 547 95 14 Ⓜ Plaza de España

FELIX ANTIGÜEDADES

An antiques shop in the heart of the Rastro flea market where you'll find an intriguing collection of *objets d'art*. Felix Antigüedades' specialities are Oriental art and musical instruments.

✛ D10 ✉ Plaza General Vara del Rey 3 ☎ 91 528 49 30 Ⓜ La Latina

GALERIAS PIQUER

This pleasant mall in the Rastro street market has 20 antiques shops. Try Siglo 20 for art deco, and El Estudio, which sells Isabelline furniture and lamps.

✛ bIII; D9 ✉ Calle Ribera de Curtidores 29 Ⓜ La Latina

EL GATO NEGRO

There's shelf after shelf of every conceivable type of knitting wool, yarn, silk, and cotton in this lovely old-fashioned shop, along with accessories of all kinds for knitters, crochet addicts, and embroiderers.

✛ bII ✉ Plaza Mayor 30 (entrance on Calle de Postas) ☎ 91 366 58 00 Ⓜ Sol

MUSEO THYSSEN-BORNEMISZA

Arguably the best of the museum shops, with reproductions of the paintings in the collection, silk scarves, ties, mugs, bags, posters, and books, all on an artistic theme.

✛ dII; E9 ✉ Paseo del Prado 8 ☎ 91 420 39 44 Ⓜ Banco de España

NUEVAS GALERÍAS

The third antiques mall in the Rastro street market, with 15 stores. Everything from brass to restored furniture, paintings, prints, and *objets d'art*.

✛ bIII; D9 ✉ Ribera de Curtidores 12 Ⓜ La Latina

WHERE TO GO

Madrid's amazing array of antique shops are in three main areas: the *barrio Salamanca*, around the Calle del Prado and Santa Ana, and around the Rastro, particularly down the Calle Ribera de Curtidores–the most likely source for bargains. Many shops do not specialize and sell a broad selection of merchandise.

Offbeat & Unusual

WHAT'S ON OFFER?

The little specialist shops of Madrid can offer much insight into the minds of the city's inhabitants. Sometimes the shop's layout is so irrational that it is hard to know what the place is really selling. You would not actually want to buy anything at some of these places—it's junk. Particularly in the area around the Plaza Mayor, the district of La Latina, and the area between Calle del Barco and Calle Hortaleza, just off the Gran Vía, it is worth pausing to admire off-beat window displays. These have been lovingly put together by proprietors who know they are as much a part of the urban landscape as any monument.

ALMIRANTE 23

This amazing little shop is a collector's dream—postcards, cinema programmes, menus, tobacco tins, sunglasses, they're all here. If you can't find what you're looking for, you can leave a forwarding address.

➕ E8 ✉ Calle Almirante 23 ☎ 91 308 12 02 🚇 Chueca

EL ARCO DE CUCHILLEROS

Following the centuries-old tradition of handicrafts on Plaza Mayor, this modern cooperative of Spanish artists turns out high-quality jewellery, pottery, textiles, *mantones* (shawls), and more.

➕ bll ✉ Plaza Mayor 9 ☎ 91 365 26 80 🚇 Sol

LAS BAILARINAS

Designer Monica García's brightly painted shoes are the talking point of this Chueca store which also sells bags, belts and other fashion accessories.

➕ dl; E8 ✉ Calle Piamonte 19 ☎ 91 319 90 69 🚇 Chueca

BELLOSO

Madrid is famous for shops specializing in religious objects—rosaries, statues, crib pieces, paintings, icons, altar lamps etc. This emporium is just off Plaza Mayor.

➕ bll; D9 ✉ Calle Mayor 23 ☎ 91 336 22 58 🚇 Sol

CARAMELOS PACO

Devoted exclusively to candy, Caramelos Paco sells sugary replicas of elephants, rabbits, and a village square; the window display is unique.

➕ blll; D9 ✉ Calle Toledo 55 ☎ 91 365 42 58 🚇 La Latina

CASA HERNANZ

This rope shop specializes in espadrilles (rope-soled shoes), but you'll also find other handmade items including mats and light shades, wooden picture frames, and woven baskets.

➕ bll ✉ Calle Toledo 18 ☎ 91 365 36 85 🚇 Sol

CASA JIMÉNEZ

The *mantillas* and shawls around the shoulders of Spanish women of a certain age are one of their distinguishing dress features. Casa Jiménez has been selling them since 1923.

➕ bll; D9 ✉ Preciados 42 ☎ 91 548 05 26 🚇 Callao, Santo Domingo

EXPRESIÓN NEGRA

Recycled drink cans are transformed into eye-catching CD racks, briefcases, and boxes in this shop specializing in African arts and crafts. Also sells handmade toys, woven baskets, rugs, and colourful patchworks.

➕ dl ✉ Calle de Piamonte 15 ☎ 91 319 95 27 🚇 Chueca

HOMELESS

This boutique was founded in 1994 in San Sebastian as a fund-raising venture for the homeless. It now has its own label, "HOSS." The designs are casual, but stylish, aimed mainly at young professionals. There's another branch in the Salamanca district (Calle Serrano 16).

www.homeless.es
✚ cl; D7–8 ✉ Calle Fuencarral 16 ☎ No phone ⓜ Gran Via

LUIS VILLASANTE

Luis Villasante specializes in material for religious habits and gives saints' names to its various shades of cloth—dark brown is "Saint Francis of Assisi." Other religious artefacts are also available and the window display, full of models of Baby Jesus, is fascinating. You'll find similar fare at El Angel "Sobrinas de Pérez" further along Calle Postas.
✚ bll; D9 ✉ Calle Postas 14 ☎ 91 366 46 40 ⓜ Sol

PALACIOS Y MUSEOS

This unusal shop sells items otherwise only available from museums, both international and Spanish. Everything is made by the same company that supplies the museums.
✚ F8 ✉ Calle Velázquez 47 ☎ 91 577 42 01 ⓜ Velázquez

PERFUMERIA ALVAREZ GÓMEZ

There are branches of this long-established perfumery all over Madrid. They sell a huge range of cosmetics and scents, but mostly their own delicate and flowery fragrances and colognes, beautifully bottled and excellent value for money.
✚ cl ✉ Calle Sevilla 2 ☎ 91 429 66 04 ⓜ Sevilla
✚ C8 ✉ Calle Serrano 14 ☎ 91 431 16 56 ⓜ Serrano

POPLAND

An Aladdin's cave of 1950s and '60s pop kitsch, where you will find everything from Beatles' memorabilia and old James Bond film posters to novelty badges, key rings, money boxes, mugs, and even Judy Garland cut-out dolls.
✚ D7 ✉ Calle Manuela Malasaña 7 ☎ 91 446 38 95 ⓜ Bilbao

ROSA NEGRA

Come here for some of the whackiest gifts, household items, and toys on offer anywhere—everything from Simpson's mugs to inflatable skeletons. The window displays are a joy.
✚ D8 ✉ Calle Fuencarral 6 ☎ 91 531 80 80 ⓜ Gran Via

SANTERÍA LA MILAGROSA

Amulets and birth charts, tarot cards, icons, statues of the Madonna, books on white magic, candles—in short, all things spiritual—is the business of this fascinating shop behind Puerta del Sol.
www.santerialamilagrosa.com
✚ cll ✉ Calle de Espoz y Mina 5 ☎ 91 524 01 42 ⓜ Sol

SESEÑA

With a firm eye on maintaining quality control, this family establishment dating back to 1901 specializes in capes. Pablo Picasso, Michael Jackson, and Hillary Clinton have all been customers.
✚ cll; D9 ✉ Calle de la Cruz 23 ☎ 91 531 68 40 ⓜ Sol

TYPICALLY SPANISH BUYING

Madrid is the best place in Spain to buy all kinds of typically Spanish products. Consider taking home a cape, a *boina* (a typical Spanish gentleman's cap), a *bota de vino* (leather wine container, from which the wine is poured at arm's length into the mouth), a typical *azulejo* tile, or a bottle of olive oil.

Books & CDs

READING ABOUT MADRID

To get an insider's view of life in the Spanish capital, you could do worse than read Madrid novels such as Benito Pérez Galdos' *Fortunata y Jacinta*, a work of Dickensian scope and depth set in 1860s Madrid; Arturo Barea's *The Forge*, a boyhood look at life before and during the Spanish Civil War; and Camilo José Cela's *The Hive*, post-Civil War Madrid through the eyes of the 1989 winner of the Nobel Prize for Literature. Cervantes' *Don Quixote*, the great *oeuvre* of Spain's Golden Age, mentions Madrid briefly. British journalist John Hooper's *The New Spaniards* is a perceptive overview of contemporary Spain. All are available in English.

BOOKSELLER'S

The capital's best English-language bookshop also sells imported magazines and Spanish and Latin-American literature in translation. Excellent children's section.

➕ E6 ✉ José Abascal 48 ☎ 91 442 79 59 Ⓜ Rubén Dario

CASA DEL LIBRO

The House of the Book claims to stock everything. It does not, but three rambling floors do manage to give an impression of comprehensiveness. The foreign literature section in this branch is well-stocked.

➕ bl; D8 ✉ Gran Vía 29 ☎ 91 521 21 13 Ⓜ Gran Vía

CUESTA DE MOYANO

Every Sunday at 10.30 the book stalls open up along the street to the Retiro from Atocha. Many books are modern and no cheaper than in stores, but there is a smattering of second-hand books in other languages, and the occasional gem waiting to be found.

➕ E10 ✉ Calle Claudio Moyano (next to Botanical Gardens) Ⓜ Atocha

EL FLAMENCO VIVE

There is no doubt that flamenco lives inside Alberto Martínez's shop, Spain's first devoted to flamenco. In addition to a good selection of music, there are books on flamenco history and much flamenco paraphernalia.

➕ all; D9 ✉ Calle Conde de Lemos 7 ☎ 91 547 39 17 Ⓜ Opera

THE INTERNATIONAL BOOKSHOP

Madrid's only non-Spanish-language second-hand bookshop is American-owned and centrally located, and stocks far more than old paperbacks. Though most books are in English, it deals in other languages, too. Like all good bookshops, it has a resident cat, Petra.

➕ bl; D9 ✉ Calle Campomanes 13 ☎ 91 541 72 91 Ⓜ Santo Domingo, Opera

MADRID ROCK

Madrid's biggest and best record shop. Three floors stock just about everything including imports, and there are video screens, listening booths, and a ticket service. Smaller branches are in Calle Mayor and Calle San Martín.

➕ cl; D8 ✉ Gran Vía 25 ☎ 91 523 26 52 Ⓜ Gran Vía

TONI MARTIN

This music shop, specializing in country, jazz, and rock 'n' roll, stocks a great selection of CDs and vinyl, new and second-hand.

➕ C8 ✉ Calle Martín de los Heros 18 ☎ 91 542 50 20 Ⓜ Plaza España

Food & Wine

BURGOS EL PALACIO DE LOS QUESOS

The window display in the Cheese Palace is one of the capital's most mouth-watering. Established in 1919.

✚ bll; D9 ✉ Calle Mayor 53 ☎ 91 548 16 23 🚇 Sol

CAFÉS POZO

One of Madrid's Cafés Pozo stores which sells a wide range of coffees, teas and infusions blended to order.

✚ F–G5 ✉ Calle Pradillo 56 ☎ 91 415 14 38 🚇 Concha Espina

HORNO SAN ONOFRE

This *pasteleria* (cake shop) is the oldest in Madrid. Look out especailly for the customized seasonal cakes and pastries including *turron* (nougat) around Christmas time and *huesos de santos*, a marzipan confection sold at All Saints' (November).

✚ D8 ✉ Calle de San Onofre 2 ☎ 91 532 72 16 🚇 Gran Via

LAVINIA

Huge shop selling quality and affordable wines. The choice is astounding, the staff knowledgeable and helpful.

✚ F7 ✉ Calle José Ortega y Gasset 16 ☎ 91 426 06 04 🚇 Nuñez de Balboa

MALLORCA

This branch of the reputable delicatessen chain offers a mouth-watering selection of cheeses, hams, pastries, filled rolls, seasonal cakes, and ice-creams. There's a small counter where you can sample before you buy.

✚ E8 ✉ Calle Serrano 6 ☎ 91 577 18 59 🚇 Retiro

MUSEO DEL JAMÓN

Each of the city's five branches of the Ham Museum is a spectacular testament to the fact that vegetarianism in Spain has a long way to go. *Jamón serrano* is the most popular, while *jamón de Jabugo* is the crown jewel.

✚ cl; E9 ✉ Carrera de San Jerónimo 6 ☎ 91 521 03 46/57 21 🚇 Sol

NIZA

Step back in time in this traditional 19th-century *patisserie* with stuccoed ceiling, marble counter, and wooden fittings. The confections on sale are equally attractive— delicious cakes, pastries, biscuits, and sweets.

✚ E8 ✉ Calle Argensola 24 ☎ 91 308 13 21 🚇 Alonzo Martinez

PATROMONIO COMUNAL OLIVARERO

There's a fabulous range of olive oil from all over Spain at this fashionable shop, including some varieties unobtainable elsewhere. Great presents to take home.

✚ E7–8 ✉ Calle Mejia Lequerica 1 ☎ 91 308 05 05 🚇 Alonzo Martinez

RESERVA Y CATA

Don't miss this *bodega* (wine store) in a Chueca basement offering 600 different wines of mainly Spanish origin.

✚ dl; E8 ✉ Calle de Conde de Xiquena 13 ☎ 91 319 04 01 🚇 Colon

WINE, CHEESE, AND *CHORIZO*

Spanish wine is slowly acquiring an international reputation, but Spanish cheese is not, although much of it is very good. The most typical is Manchego, which varies tremendously in quality, while the strongest is Cabrales, made from a mixture of sheep's and goat's milk. In addition to the hams, the Spanish sausages known as *chorizos* and the *morcill* (black pudding or blood sausage) are worth sampling.

Opera & Classical Music

ZARZUELA

In the words of Edmundo de Amici, writing in 1870, the *zarzuela* is "a piece of music somewhere between comedy and melodrama, between opera and vaudeville, with prose and verse, both recited and sung, serious and light-hearted, a very Spanish and very entertaining musical form." Among theatre audiences of a certain age, it remains as popular as ever.

AUDITORIO NACIONAL DE MÚSICA

Madrid's finest classical music venue is home to the Spanish National Orchestra, the ONE. It runs several seasons each year, the most important of which is the ONE's own October–June season. Good acoustics in circle seats.
🚇 F5 ✉ Príncipe de Vergara 146 ☎ 91 337 01 00 🚇 Cruz del Rayo

CENTRO CULTURAL DE LA VILLA

A multi-arts complex that occasionally offers classical recitals by visiting international musicians in contemporary design surroundings.
🚇 E8 ✉ Plaza de Colón ☎ 91 480 03 00; tickets: 902 10 12 12 🚇 Colón

CIRCULO DE BELLAS ARTES

This is the best forum for contemporary classical music, with its own ensemble, the Grupo Círculo.
🚇 dII; E9 ✉ Calle Marqués de Casa Riera 2 ☎ 91 360 54 00; theatre: 91 532 44 38; tickets: 902 22 16 22 🚇 Banco de España

FUNDACIÓN JUAN MARCH

Sponsors a regular lunchtime programme of chamber concerts and recitals (starting around midday and usually free), along with world-class art and sculpture exhibitions.
🚇 F7 ✉ Castelló 77 ☎ 91 435 42 40/48 40 🚇 Nuñez de Balboa

LA CORRALA

La Corrala is used as an open-air *zarzuela* location for performances in summer.
🚇 dIV; D10 ✉ Calle Tribulete 12 ☎ No phone: see press for details 🚇 Lavapiés

TEATRO MONUMENTAL

The place where classical concerts are recorded for broadcast by the Spanish Radio and Televison Orchestra and Choir.
🚇 cIII; E9 ✉ Calle Atocha 65 ☎ 91 429 12 81/902 33 22 11 🚇 Antón Martín

TEATRO PRADILLO

The best venue in Madrid for world music and anything else off the musical beaten track. Improvisation evenings and performance art.
🚇 G5 ✉ Calle Pradillo 12 ☎ 91 416 90 11 🕙 See press for details 🚇 Concha Espina

TEATRO REAL

The grandest and most beautiful of the European opera houses.
www.teatro-real.com
🚇 aII; C9 ✉ Plaza de Isabel II ☎ 91 516 06 06/902 24 48 48 🚇 Opera

TEATRO DE LA ZARZUELA

Zarzuela is the *raison d'être* for this beautiful 1,300-seat hall. While the Teatro Real was under renovation, it was also Madrid's official opera house, but now also hosts ballet and lesser known operatic works not found at the Real.
🚇 dII; E9 ✉ Calle Jovellanos 4 ☎ 91 524 54 00; tickets 902 22 16 22 🚇 Banco de España

Flamenco, Rock & Jazz

BAR CAFÉ DEL FORO
Though it does mount straight rock, the Café del Foro also has salsa, fusion, and cabaret as well as occasional magic and comedy shows. Friendly and buzzing venue.

➕ D7   ✉ Calle San Andrés 38   ☎ 91 445 37 52   🚇 Bilbao

CAFÉ CENTRAL
One of the best jazz venues in Europe. There are performances every night mainly from Spanish, but sometimes foreign, musicians.

➕ cIII; D9   ✉ Plaza del Ángel 10   ☎ 91 369 41 43   🕐 Daily 10:30PM   🚇 Sevilla, Antón Martín, Sol

CAFÉ POPULART
Live music every day—jazz, blues, and swing—in a comfortable environment where the conversation is always intelligent.

➕ cII; E9   ✉ Calle Huertas 22   ☎ 91 429 84 07   🚇 Antón Martín

LAS CARBONERAS
Madrid's newest flamenco club is already rated by aficionados for its quality acts. The show begins around 11PM, but arrive earlier if you want to be sure of a seat. The restaurant serves snacks and meals.

➕ bII   ✉ Calle del Conde de Miranda 1   ☎ 91 542 86 77   🚇 Sol

CASA PATAS
The best-known of Madrid's flamenco *tablaos* is a little touristy but none the less enjoyable. Live midnight performances, more frequent in May.

➕ cIII; D9   ✉ Calle Cañizares 10   ☎ 91 369 15 74/04 96   🕐 Thu–Sat midnight   🚇 Tirso de Molina, Antón Martín

CLAMORES JAZZ
Jazz is still at the heart of this elegant *bôite* but it now features tango and even karaoke. Live music each night.

➕ D7   ✉ Calle Alburqerque 14   ☎ 91 445 79 38   🕐 Daily 10PM   🚇 Bilbao

LA RIVIERA
One of Madrid's main rock venues, known for its good acoustics, and it's easy to see the stage. Another plus is the articulated roof which can be drawn back on hot summer nights. See listings magazines for concert details.

➕ C10–11   ✉ Paseo de la Virgen del Puerto   ☎ 91 365 24 15   🚇 Piramides

EL SOL
Chaotic and a bit shabby, but lots of fun, El Sol was big in *movida* Madrid. You'll find a wide mix of music. Central location.

➕ cI; D9   ✉ Calle Jardines 3   ☎ 91 532 64 90   🚇 Sol, Gran Via

SURISTÁN
The live music in this modern bar comes from around the world and ranges from hip-hop to flamenco. The club-like atmosphere attracts a friendly, cosmopolitan crowd. Concerts start around 10PM. Closed Mon www.suristan.com.

➕ D7   ✉ Calle de la Cruz 7   ☎ 91 532 39 09   🚇 Sevilla

MORE ROCK THAN FLAMENCO

Madrid's rock venues continue to offer lucky visitors the chance to see performers who usually play much larger places, in relatively intimate surroundings. Prices of tickets are not unreasonable, although you might not say the same of drinks. Surprisingly, there are few flamenco bars.

81

Late-Night Bars (Cervecerías)

MADRID BY NIGHT

With almost 4,000 places to have a drink, Madrid can claim to be Europe's finest city for sheer variety of late-night options—sometimes very late indeed. Main bar areas in the centre are the start of the Paseo de la Castellana (sophisticated), Malasaña (thoroughly unsophisticated), La Latina and Santa Ana (somewhere in between), and Chueca (gay).

ALHAMBRA

This bar is a good place to start an evening on the town. The Andalucian *tapas* are recommended. Around 11PM the lights dim and customers are asked to leave their tables and drink at the bar.
➕ dl ✉ Calle Victoria 9 ☎ 91 521 07 08 🚇 Sol

LA BOCA DEL LOBO

"The Jaws of the Wolf" is a lively dance bar where the music can be anything from hip-hop to rock 'n' roll, depending on the DJ. Dark, smoky atmosphere. Open from 10PM till late.
➕ dl ✉ Calle Echegaray 11 ☎ 91 429 70 13 🚇 Sevilla

CAFÉ MANUELA

After being wowed by the decor, visitors usually find the congenial atmosphere here well-suited to writing postcards or chatting to friends. Occasional live entertainment—music concerts, poetry readings, exhibitions by local artists.
➕ D8 ✉ San Vincente Ferrer 29 ☎ 91 531 70 37 🚇 Tribunal

CERVECERÍA ALEMANA

One of the city's most popular bars. A good meeting place in the Santa Ana district.
➕ cll; D9 ✉ Plaza de Santa Ana 6 ☎ 91 429 70 33 🚇 Antón Martín

LA COQUETTE

The only Madrid bar dedicated exclusively to blues is very 1960s and very studenty.
➕ D9 ✉ Calle de las Hileras 14 🚇 Opera

LA CRIPTA MÁGICA

A little off the beaten track and a little offbeat— the drinks come with a magic show. For a long time, entry was by password only, but now the place is open to all.
➕ dIV; E10 ✉ Calle de Tarragona 15 ☎ 91 539 96 96 🚇 Palos de la Frontera

FINNEGAN'S

Of the several Irish bars and clubs in Madrid, this unpretentious favourite comes the closest to authenticity. Fixtures and equipment are imported—the bar used to be the counter of a textile shop in County Cork.
➕ E8 ✉ Plaza de las Salesas 9 ☎ 91 310 05 21 🚇 Chueca

LOS GABRIELES

Decorated throughout with stunning *azulejos* (tiles). Around 11PM tables are packed away and it becomes more like a nightclub, with a DJ at weekends. Flamenco on Tuesday evenings.
➕ dl ✉ Calle Echegaray 17 ☎ 91 429 62 61 🚇 Sevilla

LIBERTAD 8

A very relaxed watering-hole with nightly cabaret, plenty of seating, and lots of cigarette smoke.
➕ dl; E8 ✉ Calle Libertad 8 ☎ 91 532 11 50 🕐 Daily 11.30PM 🚇 Chueca

VIVA MADRID

The tiled *azulejo* frontage of Viva Madrid has been photographed for a thousand guide books.
➕ cll; D9 ✉ Calle Manuel Fernández y González 7 ☎ 91 429 36 40 🚇 Antón Martín

Terrazas & Cocktail Lounges

CAFÉ RUIZ

A relatively peaceful retreat from the night-time mayhem of the surrounding *barrio* of Malasaña, the Ruiz retains a late 19th-century feel and serves cocktails as well as coffee and milkshakes

✚ D7 ✉ Calle Ruiz 11 ☎ 91 446 12 32 🚇 Bilbao

EL CHICOTE

Opened in 1931, El Chicote is the granddaddy of Madrid's *coctelerías* (cocktail bars) and continues to be a nocturnal reference point for the rich and famous. Art deco fixtures and alcove seating. Legend has it that the Chicote's *mojito* was Ernest Hemingway's favourite tipple. Memorable, if rather expensive.

✚ bl; D8 ✉ Gran Vía 12 ☎ 91 532 67 37 🚇 Gran Vía

LE COCK

Round off the evening with a cocktail or two beneath the glass roof of this tastefully decorated late-night bar.

✚ dl ✉ Calle Reina 16 ☎ 91 532 28 26 🚇 Banco de España

DEL DIEGO

Del Diego's superb design and highly attentive bar staff have quickly made it one of Madrid's big three *coctelerías*, along with El Chicote and Le Cock, two minutes away. This is the place to be or be seen.

✚ cl; E8 ✉ Calle de la Reina 12 ☎ 91 523 31 06 🚇 Gran Vía

FORTUNY

Glitzy nightclub where you might bump into media celebrities who happen to be in town. The terrace garden is the best feature of this former palace, which also has a reputable restaurant serving Mediterranean cuisine. Strict dress code.

✚ D7 ✉ Fortuny 34 ☎ 91 319 05 88 🍴 Closed lunch Sat–Sun in winter 🚇 Bilbao

EL PABELLÓN DEL ESPEJO

Back in the 1980s this lively thoroughfare was known as "Recoletos Beach" because of the number of people sunning themselves on the café terraces. Most have now disappeared, but you can recapture the atmosphere in this elegant pavilion which sells a selection of *tapas* and *raciones* (snacks), as well as drinks.

✚ D7 ✉ Paseo de Recoletos 31 ☎ 91 319 11 22 🚇 Banco de España

PASEO DE PINTOR ROSALES

The *terrazas* here run along the side of the Parque del Oeste. Noisy and lots of fun.

✚ C8; C7 ✉ Paseo de Pintor Rosales 🍴 Apr–Oct 🚇 Plaza de España, Ventura Rodríguez

PLAZA DE CONDE DE BARAJAS

Just behind the Plaza Mayor, away from the traffic, and without music, this is the most peaceful of the *terrazas*. Open only in summer.

✚ bll; D9 ✉ Plaza de Conde de Barajas 🚇 Sol, Opera

TERRAZAS

Young *madrileños* go to *terraza* bars (that is, just about any bar with chairs and tables outside) to show off their suntans and drink late into the night. It is entirely logical that between April and late October, with temperatures around 30° Centigrade (the upper 80s Farenheit), bar culture should move outside, and the streets and squares are hectic and fun.

83

Clubs & Discos

RAVE ON

The limitless capacity of *madrileños* for having fun has made Madrid a dance club owner's dream. The city is the undisputed European nightlife capital, and the night begins and ends very late indeed.

BERLÍN CABARET

There are shades of Lisa Minelli in this cabaret club where the performers include singers, magicians, and drag acts. The website has a calendar of events.
www.berlincabaret.com
⊞ alll ⊠ Costanilla de San Pedro 11 ☎ 91 366 20 34 🕐 11pm–5am (Fri–Sat till 6am) 🚇 La Latina

CAFÉ LA PALMA

A cross between a conventional café, a wine bar, a Moroccan tea shop, and a nightclub, the music in La Palma is just as eclectic—everything from rock 'n' roll to flamenco and Cuban fusion.
⊞ D8 ⊠ Calle de la Palma 62 ☎ 91 522 50 31 🕐 Daily from 4pm 🚇 Noviciado

CHESTERFIELD CAFÉ

Bands from Europe and the US perform rock and blues live from Wed–Sat in this American-style café-bar, which serves hamburgers and French fries, ribs, and pasta dishes. Good choice of beers and cocktails.
⊞ D8 ⊠ Calle Serrano Jover 5 ☎ 91 542 28 17 🚇 Argüelles

EMPIRE

The space is original with five bars on two floors: from above you look down on the people dancing. The clientele is in the 25 to 35 age group.
⊞ dl; E8 ⊠ Paseo de Recoletos 16 ☎ 91 431 54 27 🚇 Colón

GARAMOND

A chic disco in the fashionable Salamanca district, Garamond's castle-like interior attracts actors and other celebrities. Strict door policy and dress code.
⊞ F8 ⊠ Calle de Claudio Coello 10 ☎ 91 587 19 74 🚇 Retiro

JOY ESLAVA (MADRID)

Plush, though not forbiddingly stylish, in an 1850s theatre. The central location attracts a diverse clientele.
⊞ bll; D9 ⊠ Calle Arenal 11 ☎ 91 366 37 33 🚇 Ópera

KAPITAL

Macro-disco with two huge dance floors, playing various kinds of music. In the same building you'll find a karaoke bar, a fast-food restaurant, and a cinema.
⊞ dlll–IV ⊠ Calle Atocha 125 ☎ 91 420 29 06 🕐 12am–5am (weekends from 7pm). Closed Sun and Wed 🚇 Atocha

PALACIO DE GAVIRIA

One of Madrid's more remarkable night-time locations. An 1851 palace, with fixtures and furniture generally intact, it reopened in 1981 as a nightspot. With its grand staircase entrance and 14 halls it is well worth checking out.
⊞ bll; D9 ⊠ Calle Arenal 9 ☎ 91 526 60 69 🚇 Sol

PACHÁ

The mix of styles at this disco is wild and wonderful and the dance music hard and driving. Popular central location.
⊞ D8 ⊠ Calle de Barceló 11 ☎ 91 447 01 28 🚇 Sol

Cinemas

ALPHAVILLE

Alphaville opened shortly after democracy came to Spain. It shows international films in original versions with Spanish subtitles. Late-night showings on weekends and a good café downstairs.

➕ C8 ✉ Calle Martín de los Heros 14 ☎ 91 559 38 36 Ⓜ Plaza de España

FILMOTECA ESPAÑOLA

Inaugurated in 1922 as the Cine Doré and lovingly re-created in 1989, the Filmoteca shows four original-version films daily in two theatres. Many films are classics, others are truly obscure, but most are worth taking a chance. Tickets may be three times cheaper than anywhere else. A good bookshop and a pleasant bar are in the foyer.

➕ cIII; E9 ✉ Calle Santa Isabel 3 ☎ 91 467 26 00 Ⓜ Antón Martín

IDEAL YELMO CINEPLEX

Madrid's most comfortable cinema has eight theatres of varied size showing art and mainstream features. Weekend late-night showings.

➕ cIII; D9 ✉ Calle Doctor Cortezo 6 ☎ 91 369 25 18/03 31 Ⓜ Sol, Tirso de Molina

IMAX

Madrid's IMAX cinema is a great place to take the children (6 years upwards) to see spectacular wildlife and National Geographic documentaries. There are two screens—the 30m (98ft) diameter Omnimax and the Imax 3D where they can enjoy 3-dimensional effects through special glasses. Tickets from:
El Corte Ingles
☎ 90 240 02 22
and Servicaixa
☎ 90 233 22 11.
➕ F12 ✉ Meneses, Parque Tierno Galván ☎ 91 467 48 00 Ⓜ Méndez Alvaro

PRINCESA

Since it opened in the mid 1990s, this has become the city's main screening point for new Spanish films and a good place to sample the burgeoning local film industry.
➕ D7–D8 ✉ Calle Princesa 3 ☎ 91 541 41 00 Ⓜ Plaza de España

RENOIR

The best of the cinemas clustered around the bottom of Calle Martín de los Heros near the Plaza de España, shows the latest art films in five theatres of differing sizes. Detailed information sheets are published (in Spanish) to accompany each one. In the Plaza de España theatre there is a good film bookshop, open during the week and there are late-night showings on weekends.
➕ C8 ✉ Calle Martín de los Heros 12 ☎ 91 541 41 00 Ⓜ Plaza de España

A newer Renoir is in Cuatro Caminos.
✉ Calle Raimundo Fernández Villaverde 10 ☎ 91 541 41 00 Ⓜ Cuatro Caminos

ON THE INCREASE

While the Spanish film industry is booming, the number of cinemas is also on the increase, with 60 at last count. Most have a *día del espectador*, or audience day, which might be a Monday or a Wednesday, when tickets are half price. Always arrive well in advance for mid- and late-evening weekend showings, particularly if a film has just opened; queues start forming as much as an hour before projection time. Bigger cinemas now have advanced reservations and most have reserved seating on weekends. Movie information is published in full in all the daily newspapers: earliest showings (*pasos*) are generally at 4, latest at 10.30.

ORIGINAL VERSION

Ten of Madrid's cinemas show exclusively original-version films without dubbing:
Bellas Artes ✉ Calle Marqués de Casa Riera 2 ☎ 91 522 50 92
Rosales ✉ Calle Quintana 22 ☎ 91 541 58 00
Ideal Yelmo Cineplex ✉ Calle Doctor Cortezo 6 ☎ 91 369 25 18
Luna ✉ Calle Luna 2 ☎ 91 522 47 52

Luxury Hotels

PRICES

For a double room expect to pay:

Luxury	over €150
Mid-Range	€42–€120
Budget	under €42

Add 7 percent VAT to all prices. Many hotels in all price categories offer bargain weekend rates.

PARADORES

Spain's network of *paradores*, sumptuous aristocratic residences converted into luxury hotels, is no longer a well-kept secret, but there are none in Madrid. For information and reservations about those elsewhere ✉ Calle Requéna 3 ☎ 91 516 67 00

EL ANTIGUO CONVENTO

This hotel is a refurbished 17th-century convent and the tastefully decorated rooms overlook the cloisters and a tranquil garden.
www.elconvento.net
✚ B11 ✉ Calle de las Monjas, Boadilla del Monte ☎ 91 632 22 20 🚌 514

CASA DE MADRID

A short walk from the Royal Palace, this newly opened, exclusive hotel is owned by art historian and interior designer, Marta Medina Muro. Each room is exquisitely decorated and furnished, some with antiques.
www.casademadrid.com
✚ a1; D9 ✉ Calle Arrieta 2 ☎ 91 540 11 00 🚇 Opera

EUROBUILDING

With 600 rooms and twin towers, this is the largest hotel in Madrid. Located at the non-touristy, business end of the city, Eurobuilding is part of a complex with shops, clubs, cafés, a gym, and sauna.
www.nh-hoteles.com
✚ F4 ✉ Calle Padre Damián 23 ☎ 91 345 45 00, fax 91 531 31 27 🚇 Cuzco

GRAN HOTEL REINA VICTORIA

Facing the Teatro Español in the heart of the buzzing Santa Ana district, the magnificent 201-room Reina Victoria has historical connections with the bullfighting world.
www.trypreinavictoria.solmelia.com ✚ Cll–D9 ✉ Plaza de Santa Ana 14 ☎ 91 531 45 00, fax 91 429 4036 🚇 Sol

PALACE

Long in competition with the Ritz as Madrid's best central hotel, the 440-room Palace is a little less formal and is popular with visiting celebrities.
www.palacemadrid.com ✚ dll; E9 ✉ Plaza de las Cortes 7 ☎ 91 360 80 00, fax 91 360 81 00 🚇 Banco de España

RITZ

Spain's first luxury hotel, opened in 1910 and lives up to its name with 152 luxurious rooms in Belle Epoque style. Between spring and autumn there's a delightful terrace-restaurant.
www.lemeridien-ritzmadrid.com ✚ dll; E9 ✉ Plaza de la Lealtad 5 ☎ 91 901 67 67, fax 91 701 67 76 🚇 Banco de España

SANTO MAURO

This small hotel in the French-style former palace of the dukes of Santo Mauro has a lovely patio entrance and a swimming pool. The 37 avant-garde rooms are all fresh and inviting.
www.ac-hoteles.com
✚ E7 ✉ Calle Zurbano 36 ☎ 91 319 69 00, fax 91 308 54 77 🚇 Rubén Darío

VILLA MAGNA

With French neoclassical decor and the excellent restaurant (Berceo), the 164-room Villa Magna is favoured by visiting business people for its location at the start of the Castellana.
✚ E7 ✉ Paseo de la Castellana 22 ☎ 91 576 75 00, fax 91 575 95 04 🚇 Rubén Dario

Mid-Range Hotels

AROSA

Very central, the 139-room Arosa has long been popular, particularly with families, and makes an excellent base.

➕ cl; D8 ✉ Calle de la Salud 21 ☎ 91 532 16 00, fax 91 531 31 27 Ⓜ Sol

ASTURIAS

Convenient to the Puerta del Sol, the 175-room Asturias is close to the main sights and nightlife. Ask for an inside room if you're sensitive to noise.

➕ cll; D9 ✉ Calle Sevilla 2 ☎ 91 429 66 76, fax 91 429 40 36 Ⓜ Sevilla

CARLOS V

The 67-room Carlos V is clean and bright and is next to the Puerto del Sol. If you can get a room on the sixth floor, you will get a balcony.

➕ bll; D9 ✉ Calle Maestro Vitoria 5 ☎ 91 531 41 00, fax 91 531 37 61 Ⓜ Sol

CONDE DUQUE

Giving onto an enclosed square, the 143-room Conde Duque is among the more peaceful hotels near the city centre.

➕ D7 ✉ Plaza del Conde Valle Suchil 5 ☎ 91 447 70 00, fax 91 448 35 69 Ⓜ San Bernardo

GREEN EL PRADO

In this lovely building within easy reach of the Prado and the Santa Ana district, windows are double-glazed, ensuring a good night's sleep.

➕ cll; E9 ✉ Calle Prado 11 ☎ 91 369 02 34, fax 91 429 28 29 Ⓜ Antón Martín, Sevilla

GALIANO RESIDENCIA

In a quiet location, the Galiano's 29 spacious rooms and old-world feel make it one of Madrid's better-kept secrets.

➕ E8 ✉ Calle Alcalá Galiano 6 ☎ 91 319 20 00, fax 91 319 99 14 Ⓜ Colón

INGLÉS

The clean, 58-room family-owned Inglés is pleasantly located in a maze of narrow streets within easy reach of many sights. Good value.

➕ cl; D9 ✉ Calle Echegaray 8 ☎ 91 429 65 51, fax 91 420 24 23 Ⓜ Sevilla

MÓNACO

The Mónaco retains much charm, particularly in its intimate lobby, and some of its 32 rooms are supremely kitschy.

➕ dl; E8 ✉ Calle Barbieri 5 ☎ 91 522 46 30, fax 91 521 16 01 Ⓜ Chueca

OPERA

Rather plain-looking hotel but an excellent location near the opera house. All 79 rooms have satellite TV, some with balconies overlooking old Madrid.

➕ bl ✉ Cuesta de Santo Domingo 2 ☎ 91 541 28 00, fax 91 541 69 23 Ⓜ Opera

SUECIA

The 128 rooms are on the small side but pleasant enough. There's a terrace on the 7th floor, while the café/restaurant has a good priced *menú del día*. www.hotelsuecia.com

➕ dll ✉ Calle Marqués de Casa Riera 4 ☎ 91 531 69 00, fax 91 521 71 41 Ⓜ Banco de España

RESERVATIONS

Madrid has many hotels, and finding a room should not be hard except in tourist areas. Book as far in advance as possible, and call to reconfirm. If you arrive without a reservation, contact the accommodation agency called Brújula (✉ Head Office: Calle Princesa 1, 6th floor ☎ 91 559 97 05/9–7), which reserves rooms in Madrid hotels for a small fee. The phone is often busy, so go in person either to the head office or to one of the branches. They're at Atocha (Ⓒ 8AM–10PM) and the Chamartín Railway Station (Ⓒ 7AM–11.30PM).

Budget Accommodation

It is worth remembering that at the lower end of the scale, a good *hostal* may be more comfortable than a poor hotel. All the places on this page are *hostales*. Prices can vary according to season.

EUROPA

Offering slightly more than the average budget hotel, including hair-dryers and satellite TV. All rooms have private bath.

✚ C8 ✉ Calle del Cármen 4 ☎ 91 521 29 00 🚇 Callao

KRYSE

Two *hostales* in one, offering good value for their location just off Gran Vía. All rooms are spotless, reasonably sized and have ensuite bathroom, TV and ceiling fan. Those overlooking the street can be noisy.

✚ cl; D8 ✉ Calle Fuencarral 25, (1st floor) ☎ 91 531 15 12, fax 91 522 81 53 🚇 Gran Vía

LORENZO

The Lorenzo is most notable for its soundproof windows. Decor is stylish and rooms comfortable.

✚ cl; E8 ✉ Calle Clavel 8 ☎ 91 521 30 57 🚇 Gran Vía

LA MONTAÑA

There are five *hostales* at this address in a relatively peaceful area east of the centre. Rooms are decent-sized and well-lit.

✚ C8 ✉ Calle Juan Álvarez Mendizabal 44 (5th floor) ☎ 91 547 10 88 🚇 Ventura Rodríguez

OLÉ INTERNATIONAL HOSTEL

This Malasaña *hostel* (open 24 hours) has a good kitchen, common room with satellite TV and internet, and lockers for valuables. Linen and breakfast are included and towels are available.
www.olehostel.com

✚ D7 ✉ Calle Manuela Malasaña 23, (1st floor) ☎ 91 446 51 65 🚇 Bilbao, Tribunal

PAZ

Some rooms of this *hostal* on a quiet street overlook a shady courtyard. It's very clean, very efficient, and very friendly.

✚ bll; D9 ✉ Calle Flora 4 (2nd floor) ☎ 91 547 30 47 🚇 Sol, Opera

RETIRO/NARVÁEZ

In these two *hostales* in the same building, all rooms have showers, but not all have a toilet. Though a little way from the centre, they are easily accessible by public transport. The Retiro has 16 rooms, the Narváez 11.

✚ F8 ✉ Calle O'Donnell 27 (5th floor derecha and 6th floor) ☎ 91 576 00 37/575 01 07 🚇 Príncipe de Vergara

RIESCO

This family-run *hostal* has 27 hotel rooms at *hostal* prices. It is just off the Plaza del Sol—you can't get much more central than that.

✚ bll; D9 ✉ Calle Correo 2 (4th floor) ☎ 91 522 26 92 🚇 Sol

TRAFALGAR

The Trafalgar, in a residential area north of the centre, is excellent value. All 48 rooms are nicely decorated in modern style and equipped with satellite TV. There's a restaurant, bar, and an indoor swimming pool.

✚ D7 ✉ Calle Trafalgar 35 ☎ 91 445 62 00, fax 91 446 64 56 🚇 Iglesia

MADRID
travel facts

ESSENTIAL FACTS

Customs regulations

- The limits for non-EU visitors are 200 cigarettes or 50 cigars, or 250g of tobacco; 1 litre of spirits (over 22 percent) or 2 litres of fortified wine, 2 litres of still wine; 50g of perfume. Travellers under 17 are not entitled to the tobacco and alcohol allowances.
- The guidelines for EU residents (for personal use) are 800 cigarettes, 200 cigars, 1kg tobacco; 10 litres of spirits (over 22 per cent), 20 litres of aperitifs, 90 litres of wine, of which 60 can be sparkling wine, 110 litres of beer.

Electricity

- The standard current is 220 volts.
- Plugs are of round two-pin type.

Etiquette

- Spaniards rarely form orderly queues, but are generally aware of their place in the service order.
- Though there are clearly marked "No Smoking" areas in many restaurants, many Spaniards smoke and their smoke fills the restaurant anyway. Smoking on buses and trains is banned.
- Stretching and yawning in public is considered vulgar.
- Do not be worried about using your voice to attract attention in bars and restaurants. Say *Oiga* (Oy-ga, literally "hear me").
- In restaurants, it can take longer to get the bill than the meal; if you're in a rush ask for the bill when ordering your final course.
- Drinks are normally paid for before you leave the bar, not on a round-by-round basis.
- Tipping is discretionary, but 10 percent is normal practice.

Money matters

- Most major travellers' cheques can be changed at banks. American Express offers best travellers' cheque rates.
- Credit cards are now accepted in all large establishments and an increasing number of smaller ones.
- There are many multi-lingual cash machines: ServiRed and TeleBanco take all major cards.

Opening hours

- Shops: 9–1.30, 5–8.
- Department stores: 9–9.
- Churches: 9.30–1.30, 5–7.30. Many only open half an hour before a service.
- Museums: considerable variation, but many close on Mondays.
- Banks: Mon–Fri 9–2; between October and May many banks open from 9–1 on Saturdays.
- Some shopping malls and small shops open on Sundays.

Places of worship

- Dress formally: don't wear shorts.
- Do not enter during Mass.
- Flash photography is not normally permitted.

Public holidays

- 1 Jan: New Year's Day
  6 Jan: Epiphany
  Good Friday and Easter Monday
  1 May: Labour Day
  2 May: Madrid Day
  15 May: San Isidro
  15 Aug: Virgen de la Paloma
  12 Oct: Discovery of America
  1 Nov: All Saints'
  9 Nov: Virgen de la Almudena
  6 Dec: Constitution Day
  8 Dec: Immaculate Conception
  25 Dec: Christmas Day

Restrooms

- Public toilets barely exist, and hygiene in bars and restaurants is not always exemplary, though paper is generally available.

Spanish National Tourist Offices Overseas

- UK: ✉ 79 New Cavendish Street, London W1W 6XB ☎ 020 7486 8077
- Canada: ✉ 2 Bloor Street West, 34th Floor, Toronto, Ontario, M4W 3EZ ☎ 416 961 3131
- US: ✉ 8383 Wilshire Blvd, Suite 956, Beverly Hills, Los Angeles, CA 90211 ☎ 323 658 7188/7192; ✉ 666 5th Avenue, New York, NY 10103 ☎ 212 265 8822

Student travellers

- TIVE offers international student cards, travel discounts and insurance. ✉ Fernando el Catolico 88 ☎ 91 543 02 08/74 12 Ⓜ Moncloa

Tourist Offices in Madrid

- Municipal Tourist Office ✉ Plaza Mayor 3 ☎ 91 366 54 77 Ⓓ Mon–Fri 10–8; Sat 10–2, 3–8; Sun 10–3
- Tourist Offices for the Communidad de Madrid ✉ Calle Duque Medinaceli 2 ☎ 91 429 49 51 Ⓓ Mon–Fri 9–7; Sat 9–1
- Tourist information is also available at Barajas Airport, Chamartín Station and in the market at Puerta de Toledo.

Women or lone travellers

- Avoid poorly lit areas and parks after dark.
- Women, particularly blondes, may attract wolf-whistles.

GETTING AROUND

Bus and metro passes

- Unless you're passing through, it's best to buy the metrobús pass, valid for 10 journeys on bus and metro and available from automatic machines and ticket booths at metro stations and tobacconists. Monthly season tickets (*abono transportes*) are available; you'll need two passport photos.
- For more information ➤ 7.

Maps

- Metro maps are theoretically available from the ticket counter.
- Travel maps can be bought at newspaper stands (*kioskos*) and picked up free of charge at El Corte Inglés (➤ 73).
- Metro platforms have street maps indicating which exit leads where.

MEDIA & COMMUNICATIONS

International newsagents

- Foreign newspapers are normally available from *kioskos* beginning at lunchtime on the day of publication, and at about twice the home price. The *kioskos* at the western end of ✉ Puerta del Sol Ⓓ 24 hours ✉ Puerta de Alcalá ✉ Plaza de Cibeles are reliable. FNAC ✉ Calle Preciados and the VIPS stores also stock a good selection of foreign press.

Mail

- Buy stamps (*sellos*) from post offices (few and far between) or tobacconists (*tabac*), indicated by a yellow and brown sign above the shop.
- Madrid's most central post office is ✉ Plaza de Cibeles ☎ 91 521 65 00 Ⓓ Mon–Fri 8AM–9.30PM; Sat 8.30–2.30
- Post boxes are yellow with two slots, one marked "Madrid" and the other for everywhere else (marked *Provincias y extranjero*).

Newspapers and magazines

- The most important daily papers are *El País* (left of centre), *El Mundo* (new right), *Diario 16*

91

(centre), and *ABC* (right of centre). The sports paper *Marca* is Spain's best-selling newspaper on Mondays. Good weekly news magazines are *Tiempo* and *Epoca*, while *El Mundo's* city guide, *Metropoli*, is published every Friday and is the best available. There is also the *Guía del Ocio* (Leisure Guide).

* *The Broadsheet*, an English-language monthly, is directed at English-speaking residents.

Telephones

* Public telephones take 1 and 2 euro coins and 2, 5, 10, 20, and 50 cent coins.
* Phone cards are available from newspaper stands; most phones do not yet accept credit cards.
* Most bars have telephones; if it is not a pay phone, you are charged according to the number of units you use.
* Telefónica (the Spanish phone company) has a huge public call office. You queue up for a cabin number, then pay afterwards at the central counter ✉ Gran Via 30 🕐 Mon–Sat 9AM–midnight Other public phones are at the Palacio de Comunicaciones in ✉ Cibeles 🕐 Mon–Sat 8AM–midnight; Sun and public hols 8AM–10PM
* Cheap rate is 8PM–8AM daily.
* To call Spain from the US dial 011 34 followed by 91 for Madrid and then the seven digit number. You must dial the provincial area codes for all numbers in Spain, even when calling from the same province. Hence all Madrid numbers must be preceded by 91.
* To call the US from Spain dial 001.
* To call Spain from the UK dial 00 34 followed by 91 for Madrid and then the seven digit number.
* To call the UK from Spain dial 00 44.

EMERGENCIES

Embassies and consulates

* Australian Embassy ☎ 91 441 60 25
* British Embassy ☎ 91 319 02 00
* Canadian Embassy ☎ 91 423 32 50
* Irish Embassy ☎ 91 436 40 93
* Italian Embassy ☎ 91 423 33 00
* US Embassy ☎ 91 587 22 00

Emergency telephone numbers

* Police (Local) ☎ 092
* Police (National) ☎ 091
* Police (Guardia Civil) ☎ 062
* Police, Ambulance, Fire ☎ 112
* Red Cross Ambulance ☎ 91 335 45 45
* Telephone Information (Spain) ☎ 1003
* Telephone Information (International) ☎ 025

Lost and Found

* Municipal Lost Property Office ✉ Plaza Legazpi 7 ☎ 91 588 43 46/44 🚇 Metro Legazpi 🕐 Mon–Fri 9–2
* For objects lost on a bus: EMT ✉ Calle Alcántara 24 ☎ 91 406 88 43 🚇 Metro Lista. Ask for *objetos perdidos*.
* For objects lost on non-metro trains, call the relevant station and ask for *objetos perdidos*.
* Report a lost passport to your Embassy.
* To claim insurance, you must obtain a *denuncio* (signed statement of loss) from a police station.

Medicines and healthcare

* Pharmacies (*farmacias*) are indicated by a flashing green cross; they are usually open 9.30–2 and 5–8. All post a list of *farmacias de*

guardia (all-night chemists) and highlight the closest ones. There is also a list in the daily papers.

- Madrid's pharmacists are often happy to let you have some prescription medicines without a prescription.

Sensible precautions

- Carry valuables in a belt, pouch, or similar—not in a pocket. Be especially wary in the crowds around Plaza Mayor, Puerta del Sol, and the Rastro.
- Don't wear bags over one shoulder.
- Do not keep valuables in the front section of your rucksack. If possible, wear your rucksack on your front on buses and trains.
- Be aware of street tricks around tourist attractions. These include distracting you in conversation, or spraying foam on your back and then offering to clean it off while someone else grabs your bag.
- Avoid parks at night.
- Try to look as if you know where you're going. Never leave valuables in car boots (trunks). Rented cars have special plates which can be identified by thieves.

LANGUAGE

- The level of English does not generally exceed "OK". Explain clearly, repeatedly, and with hand signals. Spanish is phonetic, so once you master a few basic rules, you should be understood.

Pronunciation

c before an *e* or an *i*, and *z* are like *th* in thin
c in other cases is like *c* in cat
g before an *e* or an *i*, and *j* are a guttural sound which does not exist in English—rather like the *ch* in loch

g in other cases is like *g* in get
h is normally silent
ll is similar to y
y is like the *i* in onion

- Use the formal *usted* when speaking to strangers; the informal *tu* for friends or younger people.

Courtesies

good morning buenos días
good afternoon/evening buenas tardes
good night buenas noches
hello (informal) hola
goodbye (informal) hasta luego/hasta pronto
hello (answering the phone) ¿Diga?
goodbye adios
please por favor
thank you gracias
you're welcome de nada
how are you? (formal) ¿como está?
how are you? (informal) ¿que tal?
I'm fine estoy bien
I'm sorry lo siento
excuse me (in a bar) oiga
excuse me (in a crowd) perdón

Basic vocabulary

yes/no sí/no
I do not understand no entiendo
left/right izquierda/derecha
entrance/exit entrada/salida
open/closed abierto/cerrado
good/bad bueno/malo
big/small grande/pequeño
with/without con/sin
more/less más/menos
hot/cold caliente/frío
early/late temprano/tarde
here/there aquí/allí
today/tomorrow hoy/mañana
yesterday ayer
how much is it? ¿cuánto es?
when? ¿cuándo?
where is the...? ¿dónde está...?
do you have...? ¿tiene...?
I'd like..... me gustaría...
I don't speak Spanish no hablo español

Index

CityPack
Madrid *Top 25*

Jonathan Holland was born in 1961. He moved to Madrid in 1990, having lived for five years in southern Italy. As well as being a fiction writer (his novel *The Escape Artist* was published in 1994), he teaches literature at Madrid's Complutense University and is a regular contributor of articles to various magazines.

Maps © Automobile Association Developments Limited 1997, 2000, 2005
Cover Design Tigist Getachew, Fabrizio La Rocca **Contributions to "Living Madrid"** Sally Roy
This Edition Updated by Christopher and Melanie Rice

A CIP catalogue record for this book is available from the British Library.

ISBN-10: 0 7495 4358 2
ISBN-13: 978 0 7495 4358 7

All rights reserved. No part of this publication may be reproduced, stored in a retrieval system or transmitted in any form or by any means – electronic, photocopying, recording or otherwise – unless the written permission of the publishers has been obtained beforehand. This book may not be lent, resold, hired out or otherwise disposed of by way of trade in any form of binding or cover other than that in which it is published, without the prior consent of the publishers.

The contents of this publication are believed correct at the time of printing. Nevertheless, the publishers cannot be held responsible for any errors or omissions or for changes in the details given in this guide or for the consequences of any reliance on the information provided by the same. This does not affect your statutory rights. Assessments of attractions, hotels, restaurants and so forth are based upon the author's own personal experience and, therefore, descriptions given in this guide necessarily contain an element of subjective opinion which may not reflect the publishers' opinion or dictate a reader's own experiences on another occasion. We have tried to ensure accuracy in this guide, but things do change and we would be grateful if readers would advise us of any inaccuracies they may encounter.

Published by AA Publishing, a trading name of Automobile Association Developments Limited, whose registered office is Southwood East, Apollo Rise, Farnborough, Hampshire, GU14 0JW. Registered number 1878835.

© **AUTOMOBILE ASSOCIATION DEVELOPMENTS LIMITED 1997, 2000, 2003, 2005**
First published 1997. Reprinted Jan, Jun and Dec 1998; Mar and Jul 1999. Revised second edition Dec 2000. Revised third edition 2003. Reprinted Dec 2003. This edition 2005.

Colour separation by Daylight Colour Art Pte Ltd, Singapore
Printed and bound by Hang Tai D&P Limited, Hong Kong.

The Automobile Association would like to thank the following photographers, libraries and associations for their assistance in the preparation of this book: www.euro.ecb.int/ 6 (euro notes); THE BRIDGEMAN ART LIBRARY, LONDON 39b 'King Henry VIII' by Hans Holbein the Younger, Thyssen-Bornemisza' 43 'The Naked Maja' by Francisco de Goya y Lucientes, The Prado, 49t 'The Adoration of the Magi' by El Greco, Museo Lazaro Galdiano; MARY EVANS PICTURE LIBRARY 16l, 16r, 16/17; HULTON ARCHIVE 17; MUSEO CERRALBO, MADRID 29; MUSEO DE AMERICA, MADRID 28b; SPECTRUM COLOUR LIBRARY 54; STOCKBYTE 5. The remaining photographs are held in the Association's own library (AA PHOTO LIBRARY) and were taken by RICK STRANGE with the exception of the following: MICHELLE CHAPLOW 10; JERRY EDMANSON

8tl, 13t, 21, 30, 31t, 38, 40t (DACS, LONDON), 45t, 45b, 52, 53; PHILLIP ENTICKNAP 20l, 20/21; MAX JOURDAN 1b, 6tr, 8bl, 8br, 8/9, 9tr, 9b, 10tl, 10tr, 10/11, 12t, 12l, 12r, 12/13, 13r, 14tl, 14, 14/15, 15t, 15b, 16tl, 18tl, 18tr, 18l, 18r, 19tl, 19r, 20tl, 20tr, 21t, 22l, 22r, 23l, 23r, 24t, 24r; TONY OLIVER 9cr, 11t, 24l, 57, 60.

A01992
Fold out map © Mairs Geographischer Verlag / Falk Verlag, 73751 Ostfildern
Transport map © TCS, Aldershot, England

TITLES IN THE CITYPACK SERIES

• Amsterdam • Bangkok • Barcelona • Beijing • Berlin • Boston • Brussels & Bruges • Chicago • Dublin •
• Florence • Hong Kong • Lisbon • London • Los Angeles • Madrid • Melbourne • Miami • Milan •
• Montréal • Munich • Naples • New York • Paris • Prague • Rome • San Francisco • Seattle • Shanghai •
• Singapore • Sydney • Tokyo • Toronto • Venice • Vienna • Washington DC •

Stevenson College Edinburgh
Bankhead Ave EDIN EH11 4DE